What people are

# A Brigit of Ireland Devotional
# Sun Among Stars

It is a unique challenge to bridge the ancient past with the modern, and the Christian with the Pagan, but Mael Brigde does so with ease and grace. She tells the story of Brigid through remarkable poetry that is as much prayer as it is verse. This gorgeous text could be used as a guidebook for a Brigid devotee through different holidays and times of life. A must have for all lovers of Brigid.
**Courtney Weber**, author of *Brigid: History, Mystery, and Magick of the Celtic Goddess* and *The Morrigan: Celtic Goddess of Magick and Might*

[Sun Among Stars] reflects the long and deep journey that Mael Bridge has made with Brigit in her many guises ... [Her] journey is a deeply embodied one, reflecting insights gleaned during her studies which have become a living part of her. She encourages readers/students to grasp this possibility for themselves as they engage with the material.

This work offers a portal into the mysteries of Brigit and the possibility of readers grounding her qualities of compassion, courage, love, wisdom and fearlessness in their own unique ways in their current lives.

Thank you for this important and comprehensive work.
**Dolores T. Whelan**, author of *Ever Ancient, Ever New – Celtic Spirituality in the 21st Century*, and co-founder of Brigid's Way Celtic Pilgrimage

*Sun Among Stars* is an expression of one woman's devotion to a goddess who contains multitudes. Brigit is healer and muse,

i

soul-smith, midwife at the threshold of transformation. In these pages you will find prayers to form a daily liturgy, poetic tales to tell by candlelight, woven words to reach for when the soul falters in its faith. Read them aloud. Let their internal music take you swirling through time to the hearthside of the bards. Mael Brigde is their kith and kin, and her work here is as multitudinous as Brigit herself.

**Lunaea Weatherstone**, author of *Tending Brigid's Flame: Awaken to the Celtic Goddess of Hearth, Temple, and Forge*

Mael Brigde has meticulously researched the life, myths and legends of Brigit, Goddess and Saint to create this beautiful heartfelt book of contemplative poetry. The prose in her introduction and conclusion are both eloquent and honest. We, the readers, are gifted myriad ways to rekindle the eternal flame of Brigit in our hearts and homes. Míle buíochas – a thousand thanks.

**Dr Karen Ward**, Moon Mná Ireland, co-editor of *Soul Seers - an Irish Anthology of Celtic Shamanism*, and co-founder of Brigid's Way Celtic Pilgrimage

Mael Brigde is a long-time friend and a deeply dedicated devotee of Brigid. Her work with the Daughters of the Flame has been an inspiration to me for decades, and her poetry is clear and powerful. Her writing has consistently been a beacon for me, like the sunlight upon which Brigid hung her cloak. If you love Brigid, whether as Goddess or Saint, Mael Brigde's poems will have words to deepen and broaden your connection with her.

**Erynn Rowan Laurie**, author of *Fireflies at Absolute Zero* (poetry) and *Ogam: Weaving Word Wisdom*

I have had the honor of speaking alongside her at a number of online conferences dedicated to Brigit. The last presentation of hers that I experienced was an hour-long reading of her poems, each blending into the next. It was an amazing experience that will always stay with me.

**Gemma McGowan**, Priestess of Brigit, Kells, Ireland

Mael Brigde's *Sun Among Stars* is an essential weaving together of poetic inspiration, personal experience, and Brigid herself. Having read this book, you [will] have travelled along a pathway with the author, learning about who this enigmatic and powerful goddess is not from cold facts but from the heart of someone who has a strong connection to the source. It is at once contemplative and deeply personal, educational and reflecting the evolution in understanding and belief that we all go through over time. For this alone it is an invaluable addition to the corpus of material on Brigid ... Let the goddess or the saint or simply Brigid speak to you through the author's words as you step into a deeper understanding...

From the afterword by **Morgan Daimler**, author of *Pagan Portals – Brigid Meeting the Celtic Goddess of Poetry, Forge, and Healing Well*

I can't imagine reading this poetry and remaining untouched. I can't imagine allowing this book to lie, languishing and ignored, at the back of the shelf. I can't imagine allowing this book to pass you by.

From the foreword by **Orlagh Costello**, founder of Brigid's Forge

# A Brigit of Ireland Devotional

# Sun Among Stars

# A Brigit of Ireland Devotional

## Sun Among Stars

### Mael Brigde

Foreword by Orlagh Costello
Afterword by Morgan Daimler

MOON
BOOKS

Winchester, UK
Washington, USA

JOHN HUNT PUBLISHING

First published by Moon Books, 2021
Moon Books is an imprint of John Hunt Publishing Ltd., No. 3 East Street, Alresford
Hampshire SO24 9EE, UK
office@jhpbooks.net
www.johnhuntpublishing.com
www.moon-books.net

For distributor details and how to order please visit the 'Ordering' section on our website.

Text copyright: Mael Brigde 2020
Cover art: "Jo, la belle Irlandaise" by Gustave Courbet (1866).
(Portrait of Joanna Hiffernan. Wikimedia - public domain)

ISBN: 978 1 78904 695 3
978 1 78904 696 0 (ebook)
Library of Congress Control Number: 2020942458

A CIP catalogue record for this book is available from the British Library.

Design: Stuart Davies

UK: Printed and bound by CPI Group (UK) Ltd, Croydon, CR0 4YY
Printed in North America by CPI GPS partners

We operate a distinctive and ethical publishing philosophy in
all areas of our business, from our global network of authors to
production and worldwide distribution.

# Contents

Preface   1

Foreword by Orlagh Costello   4

Introduction   6

Poems & Prayers   12

Flame Offering   12

**Poems – Hillside**

"The Truth"   15

Crossing Divides   16

Well Offering   18

Shadow Harvest   19

People of the Goddess Danu   20

All-Giving Sun, Father of Brig   22

Divine Cow   24

Brechtnat and Broicseach   25

The Wives of Dubthach   29

Daughter of the Dagda   31

Danu and the Dagda   32

Dubthach maccu Lugair   33

Brigit Meets the King   34

Red-Haired Boy   36

Death of Ruadán   38

Bean Sídhe   39

The Blood-Thirsting Band   40

Violation   43

The Well   44

Triad   45

Bird of Three Realms   46

Cill Dara – Cell of the Oak                48
Curragh Sacrifice                          50
Brigit's Garden                            51
Hidden Fire                                52
Brigit and the Madman                      53
A Night's Work                             54
Hostel                                     56
The Pig Addresses Brigit                   57
The Curragh of Kildare                     58
The Nun Who Races                          59
Hungry                                     60
Macc Da Thó's Pig                          61
My Best Horse                              62
Otherworld Gate                            63
Grove of a Goddess                         64
Nut-Fed Fish                               65
Brigit's Candle Bearer                     67
The Falcon                                 68
Bear at Imbolc                             69
Woman in the Well                          70
Fionn and Brigit                           71
Pillar Stone Fire                          72
Brigit Wakens                              73
Brigit's Pastures                          74
Booleying Time                             75
Idyll                                      77
Numinous Land                              78
Three Sisters at Drung Hill                79
Three Hags                                 81
Brigit's Oaks                              83
Sunbeam                                    85
On the Burren                              86
Ancestral Dream                            87

**Poems – Hand**

| | |
|---|---|
| Everywhere | 91 |
| One and Three | 92 |
| Multiplicity | 93 |
| Song of Brigit | 94 |
| Embody | 95 |
| Brigit in the Time Before | 96 |
| Wolves and Pigs | 98 |
| Contemplations | 101 |
| Brigit Speaks with the Sword | 102 |
| Invasions | 103 |
| At Battle's Pause | 104 |
| Death of Goibniu's Grey | 106 |
| Sovereign Goddess | 108 |
| Verb: Smith | 110 |
| Goddess of Smiths | 112 |
| Bres the Beautiful | 113 |
| Ridge of Clay | 117 |
| Three Brigs and Sencha | 119 |
| Blessing Against Oppression and Submission | 121 |
| Cormac's Gift | 123 |
| Pillars of the World | 126 |
| Indictment and Defense | 127 |
| To Alba | 128 |
| The Community Learns to Read | 129 |
| Old Shawly | 130 |
| Healing Goddess | 131 |
| Stand Strong | 132 |
| Shattered Dreams | 133 |
| Held | 134 |
| The Briugu | 135 |
| Womb Blessing | 136 |
| Your Feast is Upon Us | 137 |
| Hearthfire | 138 |

Fisherman's Shield                          139
A Blessing on Your Nets                     140
Healing Ways                                141
Birth Blessing                              142
History of Pain in Ireland                  143
Keeper of Cattle                            144
By Brigit's Day                             146
Cattle in Winter                            147
Bealtaine Cattle Blessing                   149
Milk, A List                                150
Wielder of the Sword                        151
Three to One                                153
Ogam Reading                                154

**Poems – Heart**
Invitation                                  157
Mother of the Saint                         158
Convert                                     160
A Woman with God                            161
Dubthach Versus the Druid                   163
Brigit and Her Sisters                      165
Appeasement                                 167
Your People                                 170
Famine Years                                172
Walk of the Brigidines                      174
Forgotten Saint                             175
Ordination of Brigit, Bishop                177
Nonbeliever                                 178
First Encounter                             179
Conversation in Queen's Park                180
Initiation                                  182
Brigit Three (Offering Prayer)              183
– I'm Asleep and Don't Waken Me –           185
Brigit's Hermit                             186

Four Corners to My Bed                              188
Praise Song                                         189
Prayer for the Dead                                 190
Pause                                               191
Brigit to the Grieving Mother                       192
Hard                                                193
Prayer with Cancer                                  195
The Blessing I Ask                                  196
That I May Share                                    198
Threshold Blessing                                  199
Family Ties                                         200
Kindling                                            201
Relighting the Flame                                202
Above Nature                                        204
Who Tends Her Flame                                 205
Visitor at the Door                                 207
Whisper/Birth                                       208
Why I Tend Your Flame                               209
Shift Day                                           211
She Receives the Flame                              212
Suffering and Compassion (Chant)                    214
Invited to the Feast                                216
Caim of Bride                                       217
Brigit Bids Farewell to Her Bishop                  218
My Life as a Bird                                   219

**Reflections in Brigit's Well**
Daily Devotional                                    233
Who is Brigit of Ireland?                           238
Saint Brigit                                        238
The Goddess(es) Brigit                              240
Goddess and Saint                                   246
Knots in the Weaving: Misunderstandings Along
     the Way                                        248

The Perpetual Flame at Kildare                         255
A Way Forward                                          259
Afterword by Morgan Daimler                            264
Glossary                                               266
Pronunciation Guide                                    286
Irish Language                                         288
Bibliography and Suggested Reading                     290
Irish Texts                                            295
Primary Lives of St Brigit                             296
Resource List                                          298
Reviews                                                298
Courses                                                298
Conferences                                            299
Music                                                  299
Brigit-Focussed Groups                                 300
Catholic Brigidine Sisters                             300
Brigit Group (Non-Flame-Tending)                       300
Flame-Tending Groups                                   300
Pilgrimages and Festivals                              301
Online Resources (Brigit)                              301
Online Resources (General)                             302
About the Author                                       303
Author Links                                           304
Acknowledgements                                       309

# Publications History

"Goddess of Smiths," in *Sun of Womanhood* edited by Monaghan and Dermot (2013).
"Brigit's Rain," in *Your Death Full of Flowers*, edited by Slippery Elm (2017).
"Brigit – Keeper of Cattle," *The Motherhouse of the Goddess* blog (12 June 2017).
"All-Giving Sun, Father of Brig," *Harp, Club & Cauldron* edited by O'Brien and Ravenna (2018).

A number of poems from *Sun Among Stars* have been published on the author's Brigit poetry blog, *Stone on the Belly* http://stonebelly.blogspot.ca.

"Brigid, keep your own fire, for the night has fallen to you."
*Topographia Hibernica* **Giraldus Cambrensis**

With gratitude to those who have honoured Brigit
and kept her tradition alive and changing over centuries.

I ask the blessings of Brigit, our ancestors, and our descendants
on this book and all of our endeavours.

May we live with grace.

# Preface

## Finding Brigit

One afternoon more than thirty-five years ago I set foot on a path that changed my life. I found a name in a book – Brigit – and a brief column of text about her. A spark was kindled and I knew I wanted more. This led me to a search for information about Brigit and connection with her that has never ceased. Though my understanding of her has grown and shifted since those first few paragraphs, I remain drawn to Brigit like a lamb to its mother.

Ever since I was a small child, I have had a room in my heart – a hermit's cell – where the door is open to fresh air and birdsong, whatever my outward surroundings. The silence of my soul as it reaches for the divine lies at its centre. Even when I have been out of balance or feeling lost, it has always been there. But I haven't always been able to sense that place in me, to find and enter it. With Brigit I am able to feel my way back home.

In the early days, living in Vancouver, Canada, there was little I could learn about her, far from her homelands in the years before the internet. But I read that she and her nuns had tended a perpetual flame and that it was extinguished a millennium later during the Dissolution of the Monasteries. The loss troubled me – both of such a powerful devotional practice and of the gathering of women who performed it.

Several years later, at the end of 1992, I organised a group called Daughters of the Flame. My aim was to rekindle that fire and nurture a greater awareness of this important saint and goddess. We lit our initiatory candle on Imbolc 1993, little knowing that on the same day in Kildare the Irish Catholic Brigidine sisters were relighting her flame, as well.

The Daughters remain committed to Brigit, each of us keeping her flame in her own way. Tending it, or keeping a well in her honour, adding our efforts to those who have preserved her places and traditions for centuries, has become common among Christians and Neo-Pagans alike. Old and nearly abandoned practices, such as weaving her cross or making her effigy and the ceremony that surrounds them, are embraced more commonly again, in Ireland and wherever her devotees live.

In contrast to those years when so little information about Brigit was available to me, today academic papers abound, books topple off shelves, poetry, meditations, paintings, sculptures, and song blossom from every Brigit-loving heart; the internet is awash with her praises. Workshops, public rituals, and classes of all sorts are built from elements of her cult.

In that mix is a confusion of opinions and interpretations, false histories and good guesses, and those of us devoted to Brigit must make our way through all of this to our own relationship with her.[1]

I have found meaning and friendship with Brigit, and with the growing movement of people who honour her, who find inspiration through her in such diverse realms: justice, healing, ecology, and much more. She has bestowed an immense blessing on our age.

## Writing Brigit

Spiritual longing is not only a desire for the divine, but for contact with our own truest selves. This is in part what fuels its intensity. For those who have that longing and are at home in an established faith, clear definitions and perceptions, inherited prayers and rituals may naturally lead them to a place of divine communion. I did not have those supports.

When I wanted to move closer to Brigit, when facing difficulty or change, I longed for contemplative writings I could reach for that would help settle me into her. Over time, I began to write what I needed to read.

Though I had written a few poems to Brigit over the years,

they began pouring out when I faced cancer in 2011. Beginning as praise poems, contemplations, pleas, they grew to encompass and celebrate many sides of her – as goddess, saint, and historical figure, as modern amalgam of the three, as a dear and ever-revealing friend. To my delight, I discovered that the act of looking deeply into Brigit is itself a form of prayer. Gazing into her world through my own experience transports me from daily life, from concerns of past and future or any sense of ill, into a place of wonder, sustenance, and courage. My hermit cell, now lined with books, replete with tales I'd longed to know, visited by Brigit in varied guises and by her devotees, is once again a place of solace and strength.

Each poem you will find here is the most faithful rendering I could make at the time of writing. Throughout, I have done my utmost to accurately portray what I have learned of her, and where possible I give notes to help the curious reader track down sources, but since many of the poems and prayers bubbled up from a spring far distant from its head, citations have not always been possible.

I offer you these poems, words cast into the green and healing pool that is Brigit in the twenty-first century. May you find some of what you are looking for among them. Drink well. For the parched soul is epidemic in our day, and Brigit has much to offer those who thirst.

## Endnotes

1.  I will discuss some of that confusion toward the end of the book in the essay, "Knots in the Weaving: Misunderstandings Along the Way."

# Foreword by Orlagh Costello

Since I was born and reared in Ireland, I was reared with Brigid. Of course, she was presented as St. Brigid, but her stories and her feast day were celebrated every year in primary school, anyway (from approximately ages 4-12 in Ireland). As such, I was an adult before I realised other people had to "discover" the saint or deity (depending on your outlook). Mael Brigde is one such discoverer. And her outlook on Brigid is perhaps because of that need for discovery. She was driven to found the Daughters of the Flame and return flame-keeping in honour of Brigid to the world. She was driven to write poetry and prayers in honour of the Being – whether saint or deity doesn't really matter in my mind, as long as, to put it bluntly, you're doing the work! She was driven to spread the word, to teach people about this most Irish of beings, for in Ireland, for generations, while Catholicism reigned supreme officially, people still kept to the old ways in small things.

Why do I say Brigid is that "most Irish of Beings"? Because of that mix. Because even in modern Ireland, there are few people who wouldn't think of her on St. Brigid's Day, Imbolc or the 1st of February. Because even now, having a Brigid's cross in the house is considered normal enough, and lucky, even if the original intention of guarding the house from fire is sometimes lost. Even now, Brigid is more commonly mentioned, thought of or prayed to than St. Patrick, and is one of our three patron saints (the third being St. Columcille, or Columba if you prefer the Latin).

Mentions of Brigid in our ancient lore are few and far between. Even in Morgan Daimler's 2015 book, *Pagan Portals: Brigid*, there are only a handful of references in what is referred to as the source material, the old Irish writings capturing tales from the Iron Age. Mostly, this leads me to think that Brigid

4

herself is happy enough not being thoroughly defined. And it takes a certain thought process to be able to follow a Being like this without worrying too much about *what* she actually is. Mael Brigde shows this through her poetry and teachings. Even in the introduction to this book, she shows through her learnings, her knowledge, her awareness that deep divisions are not always appropriate or indeed welcome. Black and white is not the way we live our lives; we live in the infinite shades of grey ... not that there is anything grey about this book.

I don't see this as a book to be read from cover to cover – although readers may want to do that and soak up the contents in one fell swoop. I see it more as a book to be picked up when needed, allowed to fall open on a random page (or perhaps not so random; Brigid is not known for her randomness!) and the lesson within absorbed. Some of the poems are short, some are long, but all will speak to a place in your heart and soul.

I can't imagine reading this poetry and remaining untouched. I can't imagine allowing this book to lie, languishing and ignored, at the back of the shelf. I can't imagine allowing this book to pass you by. Mael Brigde herself admits the ambiguity of Brigid, and she speaks to a wider Brigid than I usually experience, looking to Scotland, Wales, and further afield for inspiration and knowledge. I have said previously that there are as many Brigids as there are people who work with her: Mael Brigde has captured something for most, if not all, of them here.

Read. And in reading, allow the essence of Brigid, whether deity, saint or nun, to enter into you.

# Introduction

*Go on your knees and open your eyes and let Brigit inside.*
Irish Folklore Collection 903[1]

## Brigit of Ireland

Saint Brigit, the daughter of a slave and her master, born unfree, destined to lead Christian women and help build the church in early medieval Ireland. Three goddesses named Brigit, three sisters, daughters of The Good God, An Dagda, honoured by healers, poets, and smiths. Virgin foster-mother of Christ, friend and companion to Mary. In the midst of battle, mother of a dying son, her loss as profound as anyone's.

Woman of fire.
Woman of wells.
Protector of the desperate.
Bringer of the spring.

## Who is Brigit?

She is all of these things and many more. It is Saint Brigit whose feast day, called Imbolc or Fhéile Bhríde (Festival of Brigit), announces the subtle shift from the dark to the lighter half of the year, from fighting starvation to anticipating growth. It is when the ewes begin to lactate, the snowdrops arise, and stock is taken of what is stored to keep us fed until the harvests can begin. It is when activity bursts into our lives: preparing our tools for the work year, inviting her blessings on our homes and families, our animals and our way of life. Brigit touches the ice of winter and promises sun.

Saint Brigit is honoured at countless healing wells and wayside shrines and chapels. In her community at Kildare, a perpetual fire once again burns in her name, and through it, blessings are sought for beings and situations, for healing, for safety, for insight, for renewal. Brigit guards the weak and oppressed, and her generosity is famous; so great is it that her own father tried to send her away to protect his belongings, and her sisters in religion attempted to hide objects from her to keep them safe. But if she gives away needed food or garments, they never fail to be replaced. No one who believes suffers for her open heart.

Justice, and the realm of the poet and scholar, the wisewoman and physician, the sorcerer and the smith all fall in the purview of the goddess Brigit. She raises her voice in outcry against transgression, her heart breaks in the first keen heard in Ireland.

Looking deeply into both the saint and the goddess who carry this name, we find reflected experience that is broad enough to encompass the scope of our lives. She has made swords for war, blessed soldiers on the battlefield, and lost her traitorous son to the spear. She has welcomed the leper at her door, sending him away with her best cow and calf. She has fed the starving dog without lessening her larder. She has taken revenge on the brother who mocked and tried to force her from her virgin path, and given instruction to her spurned suitor as to where he would find a willing wife. She has suffered; she has relieved suffering. She has been indulgent; she has been stern. She bids us to find and keep our anam cara – our soul friend. She blesses the poet, the healer, and the smith as goddess; as saint she heals abundantly and her monastery grows famous for its metalwork and its illuminated manuscript.

What you have known, in some way, she has known. She has caused the woman to love her husband passionately when he appealed to her. She has forgiven the young sinner and made the foetus vanish from her womb. She has authority, intense faith, humour, and concern. She can listen as well as she can preach. And creatures, wild and tame, are disposed to do her will.

In today's world Brigit draws to herself folk of different faiths and cultures, each of whom sees in her something strengthening, something nourishing, a spark of inspiration in a challenging world. Brigit's times were no easier than our own, and it is for this reason that she can speak to us across uncounted generations.

The Brigit we know today descends from two main sources: the traditions and writings attached to an Irishwoman who became known as a saint, and a goddess or goddesses of the same name. A great deal more is known of the former than the latter, and the historical connections between the two are based on speculation rather than strong evidence. They are seen largely as one, today, whether the emphasis is on her saint or her goddess nature, though increasingly, even amongst her followers, people are beginning to distinguish between them again, to see them as closely affiliated but separate beings. Regardless of how one views Brigit, she is an anchor in the spiritual lives of thousands of people of all ages who have learned to cherish and turn to her in gratitude and need.

Many of us, from that hidden place of silence within, have thirsted for spiritual connection that is both modern in its expression and primal in its depth. We have longed for a sacred being who values all genders, who sees through female eyes even when enacting what in her time were male roles, who through her actions demonstrates not only the desire but the power to aid the oppressed, while at the same time welcoming those of every role and status. In these ways, Brigit stands out.

To have an image of her on our altars, to tend her flame or well, to open our hearts and pray in petition and reverence are joyful things. Brigit is clearly not the only goddess or the only saint, or the only woman worthy of our trust. But she is wondrous, a great companion in our spiritual lives.

## The Poems

Often in our world there is a strict line drawn between Christian and Pagan. What is meant for one can't be valued by the other. But Brigit offers us a liminal place, somewhere that is neither fully one nor the other, and as such these poems are equally an offering to the Christian and the Pagan who are willing to embrace a little of the other – the sort of person, often, who is attracted to Brigit in the first place.

The poems in *A Brigit of Ireland Devotional – Sun Among Stars*[2] represent an exploration and an evolution of understanding of Brigit. One strand traces my own spiritual journey; others explore the often-conflicting images of Brigit presented over time. These images vary in part because the materials they arise from, spanning hundreds of years of writing and tradition, are greatly in conflict with one another, but also because my own understanding of Brigit has changed over the decades. Therefore, it is not so much a primer or a textbook as an ever-shifting prism of perception and reflection.

These poems, many of which take pleasure in or at least speculate on the past, are grounded in the present day. They seek not to replicate times of which I have only a partial understanding, but to glean wisdom from them, illuminating the present. The Brigit I perceive is not the goddess who began to rise perhaps millennia ago, nor is she the medieval woman who set up religious communities in Ireland, nor the saint who hagiographers and folk tradition transformed her into. She is rooted in these beings, but she is modern, tempered by a thousand interpretations over fifteen hundred years. To know her as well as I possibly can, I delve into those places and bring her out, in all her contradictions, to the best of my ability. I have found inspiration in medieval writings (in translation), modern folk traditions, the musings of scholars, monastics, and lay followers of Brigit, as well as in my personal and immediate devotion to her. This has provided me a vantage point to see an outline of her as she has been seen, and to measure that against my own experience.

The research that has gone into these poems is as careful as it would have been for any other genre of writing I might have chosen, and I have attempted an honest representation of where she has come from and where she appears to be in modern times. It has been an education for me to seek her in so many places. I see a greater distinction now between the saint and the goddess, and I increasingly doubt that most of the associations of the one arise from the other. However, I recognise that there has been a relatively recent merging of goddess and saint, and when we address one, we are generally addressing both. You will see this blending in many of my poems.

Would I write them differently now? In places, I probably would, but I choose to leave them their integrity and carry on.

At the back of the book you'll find an extended glossary, pronunciation guide, bibliography, and a few suggestions of places to continue your search, whether it is of a scholarly or spiritual nature, as well as an afterword by Morgan Daimler. The notes to the poems are at the end of the long chapter "Poems and Prayers," which constitutes the bulk of the book and is divided into three sections: "Hillside," "Hand," and "Heart." Poems with notes are indicated with an asterisk*.

It is my hope that the glimpses of Brigit I offer you will support the movements of your own heart, your studies and explorations, and encourage peace, compassion, creativity, and contemplation – all elements of Brigit's tradition. The writing and rereading of them has continuously brought a sense of calm and joy to me, whatever the circumstances of my life. They have been a great gift. May they be a gift to you.

### Endnotes

1. "Téigí ar bhur nglúna agus foscláigí bhur súile agus ligigi

isteach Bríd." *Irish Folklore Collection* 903: 51-3. Quoted in Ó Catháin (1995) pg. 10. From a Saint Brigit's Eve tradition practiced in County Mayo.

2. "As sun shineth among stars, (so) will shine the maiden's deeds and merits." From "On the Life of St. Brigit" in *Leabhar Breac* (*The Speckled Book*). See bibliography for links.

# Poems & Prayers

## Flame Offering

In the name of the three Brigits
I light the candle of my heart
may I offer it to everyone
gentle and steady
warm and bright

# Poems – Hillside

## "The Truth"*

how many Brigits?
one or several?
daughter of the Dagda?
mother of the gods?
did she die a virgin?
or with Bres as husband
mother ill-advised Ruadán?
or with worthy Delbaeth
give birth to
Brian   Iuchar   Iucharba
whose fame shines over hills

why must I seek to tap
the cards in one neat deck?
let me throw them to the sun
to fall wherever they will

## Crossing Divides

in your world
before gods were hidden
– race pitted against race –
slaves were taken
a man might hit his wife
feuds were legal means
to make amends

yet  too
house fostered child
of distant house
child grew
knowing stranger clans as kin
woman might leave a man
– take her goods –
if he left a mark
marriage crossed the race divide
gods and nongods lay together
all lines blurred

you  Brigit
know well of this
saint –
daughter of nobleman Dubthach
daughter of Broicseach    slave
goddess –
proud woman of the Tuatha Dé Danann
wed to Bres   half-Fomorian

let us build on your foundations
build high this arc of possibility

a loaf of bread  a jug of ale
a home to tend for all
dear mother of just peace

## Well Offering

deep
deep and black the shaft of your great well
sinks through yielding earth to touch
the sídhe

bronze
bronze and fine the offerings to
goddess Brig
forged and split and given to your world

below
below the shifting winds
and rain-wet fog
below the bawling calf
and peeling yew

far below
a goddess hears and listens
we cast our bounty
deep into your well

## Shadow Harvest

who will tell the story
of the sisters Brigit
there is no harvest of tales
gathered for them
as for their saintly heir

but shadows move
in the reeds and rushes
in the ashes and in the springs
their deep voice wakens
the wild corners of the land
in herb  and bird  and beast
in the fading rhythms
of the folk

who will gather these shadows
weave for the triple goddess
the ancient three-armed cross

## People of the Goddess Danu*

in the beginning
ancestress Danu
goddess of a splendid people
spurred them to rise and conquer Ireland
face its scourges unafraid

four objects they bore
stone of Fál
cries out when touched by rightful king
always victorious spear of Lug
foster-son of captive Tailtiu
who cleared the forest with her naked hands
Nuada the king – his well-knit sword
inescapable when once unsheathed
and tool of The Dagda   All Father   Good God
cauldron that cannot be exhausted
vessel from which all walk away replete

it was this Dagda   mighty eater
rough-cut leader of his tribe
who begot the Brigits three
Brig soon wed to Bres the Beautiful

Danu's people
skilled in magic and lore of druids
Morrigán in changing shape
Ogma in warcraft
Badb in bloody prophecy
Lug in every art
Goibniu in smithing
with Lucta wright and Creidne metalworker
Dian Cécht and his children in medicine

he chanted the slaughtered to life
at the well of Slaíne

from these heroes Brigit learned
drove the smithy
filled the cauldron
healed the injured
inspired arts
put blessing over fields of war

from her kindred she was fashioned
last of them still known to us
seeing Brigit brings the Dagda
surely as the great-thewed Goibniu
knowing Imbolc leads to Lugnasad
fair festival held by Lug each year
invoking wellness brings Dian Cécht
and his children – Airmid   Miach

though the Sons of Míl invaded
though the Gael consumed the land
though the gods have softly faded
she reveals them in her hand

## All-Giving Sun, Father of Brig*

Good God
Shapeshifter
Glowing Head
Beautiful Fire
Ruddy One of Much Wisdom

Father of All

such is the vast Dagda   Brig
the one who gave you life
perfector of divine science
possessor of triads
the god of druidry
to the gods

the sun itself in heaven
able and magnanimous
he cleared twelve plains in a single night
cut the path of twelve rivers
governs weather   crops for the Tuatha Dé

by night he dwells with the dead
by day   the living
binds together winter and summer
dark and light

builder   warrior
provider and protector
he dwells in the sublimest sídhe
at Brugh na Bóinne
the Hostel of the Mound

voracious and potent
there he lay with the Morrigan
ah  he lay with many goddesses
you have half-sisters    half-brothers
throughout the land

his cauldron a huge and mighty treasure
his dreadful iron club
one end rough and one end gentle
nine men it kills in an instant
nine men in an instant revives

your father   The Dagda
who birthed in you the mighty sun of inspiration
bequeathed you the cauldron generous
ignited in you poet and healer both

## Divine Cow*

luminous white the cow who nursed you
when taken from your mother's breast

ears of silken red   eyes of warm pitch
called from the Land of Youth
by the clear-sighted druid
the sweet cow's milk the only food
you could endure

was the land below his dwelling
alive with crying mists
as she trod the hillside's quickened flanks
in answer

had the sídhe-mound quivered with new light
when you dropped to the druid's threshold
your mother's knees resounding
one on rush-strewn floor
one on naked earth without

did the cow then lift her large
and thoughtful ears
so far away and listen for your cry

## Brechtnat and Broicseach

when Brechtnat Blaithbec
contracted to wed
the man Dubthach
it was no mere year-and-a-day
but a merging of their good fortune
that she conceived

handsome as Ogma
bright as Lug
she counted up his strengths

she too held lands
rich and fruitful as an egg
with three strong chicks

she too had family
noble and large of heart
poets praised them
traced them to the Sons of Míl

Dubthach received her
with feasting and with fires
with long nights of bards' excess
and wedded love

they were contented
consulting together
on matters of the farm
seldom did he strike her
except when just

peace well reigned

till Broicseach came
daughter of Dall-brónach
of comely appearance
good-living and a good slave

two wives   not unusual

a slave who served sundry needs
common they were

but this Broicseach turned
Brechtnat's breath
to stone

delight was all he saw in her
beauty   dazzle   might
he grasped her as the Dagda
clasped the massive Morrigan
as he swam inside of Boann
sinuous goddess of the River Boyne

Dubhtach's eyes were ever on her
she who owned not even
the soul inside her bone

within the laws of jealousy
Brechtnat raised her hand
respecter of the law
she raised no knife

when a child caught
within the belly of the slave
Brechtnat demanded they be sold

cart packed
woman wrapped in woolen shawl
long-faced
the wayward husband took her off

far   far the slave-woman went
never to return
but the child within
he did not sell

poor Brechtnat would long repent her

her seed will rule your seed
the bishop sermonised
but her seed will bring good
to your descendants
though you be cursed for the wrong
you do the slave

let the name you call her
said the druid to her father
be Brigit
(for Brigit was the goddess
instilled in her)

gone now the wife
called Brechtnat Blaithbec
long gone the husband
Dubthach son of Dreimne
their graves subside
upon the sloping hill
gone the ill-used woman Broicseach
whose daughter longed to find her

but here
here amongst us
still here
the golden
towering   sparkling
Brigit flame

## The Wives of Dubthach

or ...
perhaps it was otherwise
Broicseach not a slave at all
but second wife
heaven knows those early Irish
had unions of many types

perhaps
the monks who wrote your Lives
shied
two hundred years and more hence
from such unseemly details
one making a slave of her
another a noble wife
unfettered by wives of prior
higher claim

what if
these two wives of Dubthach
rolled up their sleeves together
chattered over churns
minded each other's children
while they beat the flax

what if
the brothers of Brigit
never mentioned in the early tales
were sprung from varied loins
but all assembled
equal
in the eyes of law
in one father's house

we will never know
the story of your childhood

may it have been
a happy one

## Daughter of the Dagda*

she it was who had
two sacred cattle
Fea and Femen
and Cirb
king of rams

after each
great plains were named

with them was Triath
king of swine

among them
three demon voices
after transgression

whistling
weeping
lamentation

this was Brigit
daughter of The Good God
with her
all might in creatures
with her
wild cries in the night

## Danu and the Dagda*

sky      sun
one-eyed horseman of the heavens
he from whom all gods descend

on Danu
woman of land and rivers
The Dagda spreads his fertile rays
red fire of all knowledge
casts his essence to mingle
with her own

corn and milk seep
as dew
from her body

countless deities
are born

## Dubthach maccu Lugair*

now was the time to lead Brigit
to her suitor

he the head
of heads of fire
poet of poets
she the one
her father loved and feared

and this husband to be
his name was Dubthach  too

so many Brigits
so many Dubthachs
but only one ruler
of Brigit's life

## Brigit Meets the King*

Dubthach left his daughter
in the chariot with his sword
(already we guess how this story has to go)
rose to enter the house of Leinster's king

not grand his dwelling
like any other man's   a little large perhaps
roofed and sheltered   shining   well-kept
free of hounds and beasts
wherein was honour and welcome
offered in honeyed words

Dubthach   at his reception
told his tale then went to fetch the maid

she spied the king
poised on his high-seat
and wooden couches   not straw
on which his guests might rest

he smiled
"your father tells me it is time for him
to sell you
for you make him a pauper
when you give his wealth away"

"not his but God's" she rejoined him
noble Dubthach grimaced at her words

the good king listened
weighed their case
said

"I fear she would make me too dear to her god
and I would have to sell my back to live
let her free   friend Dubthach
let her have her god
let us see what she will do with him
in time"

resigned
her father walked to his chariot
the daughter and the king at his side
"where is my jewelled sword?" he cried
Brigit's glance reveals

on the hillside
retreating round a bend
a man in tatters bears a burden in one arm

laughs Leinster
"here my friend!
I give you mine!"

long she served her god in Ireland
many times by her the king was bargained flat
but though he never bowed inside her chapel
he bade his druid chant
protection on her name

## Red-Haired Boy

that one
– hair the colour of dried blood –
latched his mouth
to your swollen breast
– that hair
that mouth
made from you
from his half-foreign father –
drank you into himself and grew

that child
every portion of him the promise
of a king
– his father the beautiful
his grandfather the Good God
his mother
goddess of word and craft –

how could he not fall prey
to those who twisted
turned him
how could he not wish
to please his father well

yet how
how could he come before
his mother's people
before the smith who loved him
beg of him a splendid spear
seek to cut him down

when the spear refused the service

when the smith wrenched back his arm
hurled the weapon home
how could your son not fall

before him hundreds died
born again in the Well of Wholeness
that well now shattered
Ruadán remained
as he fell

lay screaming
on crimson ground
till

silence on the land

and you
how could you not upwell
as the divine river before you broke its banks
and all the horror and all the sorrow
of that awful scything
not emerge in ululation

the birth of keening
at the slaying of your son

## Death of Ruadán

withdraw   sweet Brig
to the sunlit sídhe
happy place where death
is never known

feed yourself on apples
rest beneath the singing trees

your son is dead
your spirit trampled
when he threw the faithless spear
against his kin

## Bean Sídhe*

and with this death
sorrow        shock
this great one down
face without motion
hands without work
speech      forever gone

as we stand above
our love
across a distant border
field to field
tribe to tribe
world to world
she comes

first there is shrieking
then there is wailing
then with us she weeps

the poet's song of utter loss
our hearts swept up
in Brigit's keen

## The Blood-Thirsting Band*

a band of men
a peculiarly vain and diabolical cult
says Cogitosus
roused and craving blood
bind themselves with oaths
– oaths are a mighty thing
a vow once made cannot be denied –
they venture forth
nine strong
to find their victim   shear him through

comes Brigit  hearing of their plans
these are men she knows
who pass her on the road on market days
some grunt hellos   some turn their gaze away
from this troublesome preaching nun
some greet with jolly acknowledgement
their neighbour  their now and then friend

she sets upon them
in kindly tones and gentle phrases
urges them abandon evil plans
humble hearts   repent sinfulness
some rebuff her rudely
some shuffle feet   mumble meaningless words
some have come to her for meat and milk
sheltered her from sudden rainfalls
sold good dogs to her to guard her home

they push along their way
those who must fulfill their bloody vow
Brigit raises hands and voice

pleads with heaven
that all be saved and know the truth

comes the killing

they find their prey
these nine determined men
pierce with spears
behead with swords
return in blood-drunk revelry to their homes
many witness their swaggering
weapons black with gore
Brigit sees them too

now here is the miracle
the body is not found
the men have murdered no one
their victim tills his field unaware
that he is dead
when neighbours race to tell his wife
they stumble against each other
back away in shock
to see them laugh together there

and here is Brigit
at work in her monastery
spinning wool  threading loom  brewing dyes
to make new altar cloths
pleased  contented  happy in her work
and with her God

the men repent
says Cogitosus
at the power of her prayers

but this I doubt
one or two perhaps who leaned her way already
these may yet come to her
others might shrink  bitterly defiant and in fear
but the one they meant to slay
they never slew him
and he for one grew splendid with relief

# Violation*

man   do you think to tease God
flaunt his laws so breezily
your leg across her hedge
encroaching where you know
your sex is banned

your breath defiles these flames
tended by woman bright
with bellows strong

no surprise the madness
that assails you
now you recite
to everyone you meet
this is how I blew
on Brigit's flame

## The Well*

on its surface
skims her reflected face
(no other mirror desired)

no more the red blush
of well-washed severed heads

by the healing waters
madness dampened
illness quenched
good winds called
drive fish and fishermen to meet

she drinks the dear water
cleans   protects   tends
her whole life through
the holy well

# Triad

the three who
strengthen the smith
guide the healer
set the poet afire

these are Brigit

the three who
shriek
who weep
who hiss

these are Brigit

the three
surrounding Sencha
poet and judge –
Brig the Cowless
Brig of the Judgements
Brig the Hospitaller

Brigit
one and all

## Bird of Three Realms

Brigit's swan
smooth-necked
glimmering thread
embroiders every realm
draws them nearer to each other
one to one
to one

wings whistling
strong-shouldered
she slips
from the cushioned sky
settles
on the silver-furrowed lake

with one swift push
she breasts
the unresisting glass
drifts   wings curled above her body
digs her beak in argent waters
plucks the floating cress

she hisses at the stranger
open-mouthed
shakes her coal-ridged forehead
sets her foot like blackthorn's trunk
on damp and yielding earth
feeds along the threshold
of the realms

Brigit's swan
her shape given the fleeing

gold-chained lovers
her feathers
on whom rain beads and
– harmless –
falls
are sewn together in
the poet's journey cloak
give vision flight

bird of three realms
she sees
the trembling sky
feels
the shivering waters
hears
the earth grumbling
beneath her feet

## Cill Dara – Cell of the Oak

oak of firm memory
wise oak
ancient oak

in your sacred grove
druids act
tribes gather

in oak's presence new kings
receive their rule

through you the sky above
joins the world concealed below

light and sap
sun and spring
flow in endless rhythm

in your crown
a falcon rests
loyal friend of Brigit

nearby
three black-cloaked
grey-cowled crows

caterpillars taste
your new sprung leaves
blue tit feeds her young
your fuzzy foe

on your trunk

figure of a mighty warrior
like a mouse   treecreeper climbs
beware it
little beetle in your bark

among your roots the capercaillie
feathered horses of the woods

your acorn mast
great pigs covet

your shade
the hermit loves

surrounded by your kin
most wise of forest trees
fair Brigit dwells
to you she draws
her ever-growing host

## Curragh Sacrifice*

was it for you  Brigit  the woman was inhumed
in the centre of this banked expanse
long ago on the Curragh of Kildare

straining in her earthen grave
fighting for one breath

was she slave or noble
what did she purchase for the tribe

in the age of iron spears
golden treasures made with godlike skill
deities whose favour was not assured

what omen did the druids see that scared them so
to take a human life   most costly offering

did northern tribes press at your boundaries
the Hill of Almu under siege once more

had corn and milk grown scarce
plague creep into the rath
did she guard forever the fortune of this place

or was it what might come
promise of chaos in the flight of birds

that forced the death
of one who might have lived

# Brigit's Garden*

sweetest grass
greenest pasture
counterpart of heaven

your red-eared cattle graze
shrug off the biting fly
your wren stalks   tail alert
among the rushes' shanks
and swans breast silent on
slivers of white pond

this is your garden Brigit
where sure-footed horses
kick out chunks of earth
in delight

# Hidden Fire

within this tangled hollowed hedge
whitethorn blackthorn juniper birch
flames consume
woods of protection
woods of conjuration
strong woods of slow burn
woods of sudden snaps
and among the whispering
cackling crying woods
curl of smoke
lush and stinging
voice of sister
calmly singing

# Brigit and the Madman

the madman came
bearded and wild
toenails curved inward
hair tangled with feathers
birds dug dark beetles from his skin

seven years he'd wandered
eyes bloodied with grief for slaughter
black-pinioned spirits of battle
hung above clash and clamour
dizzied the warring chieftain
urged him to flee to woods and plain
live on cresses   take counsel from the birds

Brigit heard his gibbering
went to him with ale and butter
begged to hear the wisdom
of his unsettled mind

what did he see in her
of cress or woodcock or fawn
that permitted him to stop awhile
and preach his anguished truth

## A Night's Work

i/
so far you travel in a single night
blessing croft in Antrim
cairn in Uist
crumbled thatch in homely Faughart town

on strong legs step from the Otherworld
stride from bog to burn
quick eyes catching
– rush cross left waiting here
potato and buttermilk there
egg   winkle   straw girdle
carefully fashioned bed –

you pause
leave your print in ashes
touch each place you pass
and mark it yours

ii/
a sheaf of green rushes
left upon the flagstone

a clean bare cloak
thick-knit socks
gifts to keep you warm

you kneel
– your white cow
stands beyond –

imbue

sheaf of seed-corn
linen handkerchief
potato slits

with virtues of healing
and protection

a blessing in them now
for beast or kin

## Hostel*

your hostel
its entrance in the countryside
its contents beyond this world

vast cauldron furnishes
every sumptuous feast
wild garlic  leek
joints of tender calf
salt butter dissolves
in simmering oats

pluck of harp and lyre
mesmerising voice
games by hearthfire's glow
enrich the hours of night

a happy ageless comely place
where travellers rest
on wooden couch
and fine wool cloak

no sudden transformations
on their return without
young men turned to dust
as ages skirr

Brigit smiles on all her guests
hears their many tales
comforts them
and guides them on their way

## The Pig Addresses Brigit

simple the state I'm in
pig of Manannán Mac Lir
the god who rides a wave-born horse
his cloak the grey and frenzied
shifting sea

I am slain one day to fill
the bellies of his sídhe
alive once more the next
and slain again

Brigit
if I break for freedom
run the woodlands mad and wild
harried by hounds and hunters
chased by hungry wolves
should I make it to the Curragh
should I pound across her fields
let me mingle with your pig herds
let me end my days

in peace

## The Curragh of Kildare*

this plain
timeless
dense with industry and life
is sweet in hedge and meadowgrass
graceful long-limbed mounts at canter
peace in briskly moving breeze

here Brigit in her chariot
raced

see deeply
beneath the soil
chiefs and tribes-folk
felled by bronze and iron
land of plenty coveted by all
look there
wild land  wildlife imperilled
Hill of Allen plundered   bent
Fionn and Fianna wander here no more

yet still
you endure
– however we may understand you
whatever we may ask –
rising from spring-waters
from smallest flicker of flame
hope and comfort
in your people's hearts

## The Nun Who Races*

Cormac wrote of
the nun who races
cross the Curragh Plain

was she on foot like Macha
who cursed the Ulstermen?
or aboard her plunging chariot?

Darlugdacha at her left
reins in hand
grin split   ground tossing

and more fair sisters
two by two in flat bed carts
horses flying

cranes raise long necks
to watch
as Brigit lets loose her spear

# Hungry*

there is another side to you
goddess   saint   of our inspiration
your mouth that blew battle pipes
your earth that parted to swallow
the offered black-fringed fowl
smother her at the place
where three streams meet

we have ways to ken such things
dark forces of death   of letting go
smear of decay
from which new life unfurls
recognition of what our wills
cannot escape
or even
our own grim aspects taking root

regardless
don't think I haven't seen
this bruise-blue visage   Brigit
these hungry teeth ready to snap in two
our pretty dreams of you

# Macc Da Thó's Pig*

Macc Da Thó's pig
fine roast with forty oxen
dressed upon it

two unfriendly forces
vie for carving rights

in the bloody turmoil that ensues
they churn across the country
past Cill Dara in its silence

a stream of slaughter
through the place of oaks

## My Best Horse

this is my best horse
bones hard
from limey Curragh soil
he will bear my chariot
with all our weight
and all our visions
he with his bold
black companions
across the tracks of Éire
west and east

should our journey keep us
late upon the road
and the púca rise dripping
from the marsh
though the rest may bolt
– and God be with them –
this hard-boned lad will lock
eyes with the gravest night-mare
win us passage
our prayers and his devotion
keep straight the chariot

onward to our goal
we and he

# Otherworld Gate

open for me the gate to the Otherworld
I will enter and give thanks to Brigit
the gate through which the studious may enter
the dedicated may enter
those who submit to her fire
who open themselves to her light

I give thanks
for you have answered my sincere request
and though I was cast away
you welcomed me

you are the gate to the Land of Youth
the Land of Apples
the Land the poets seek
and you are splendid

this is the day we have striven for
I rejoice
I offer honey and ale
gifts of hospitality
justice and the keenest words of my heart

light shimmers from your noble head

boughs of juniper and birch in hand
I join the ancient procession
you are my goddess and I give thanks
you are my goddess and I exalt you
your blessings are eternal

## Grove of a Goddess*

in the dark and sacred green
oaks enlaced around   above
their bark bears the clefts
of Dagda's axe

water spills from your deep source
altar laid with sacrifice

come again the druids to this place

# Nut-Fed Fish

brown hazels ring
leaf-laced waters
nine sweet cracking maidens
elbow to elbow grow
branch twined in sisterly branch
around the sacred spring

Brigit   bestower of wisdom
drops hazel-mast
fat nut-meats
into glint-back salmons'
waiting mouths
speckles blossom
imbas grows

they who would be transformed
they who seek the second sight
they whose hearts yearn for sober
enlightenment of truth
toil for lifetimes in their poetic quest
in hope of one brief taste
of the salmon's nut-fed flesh

come the black of night-time
Brigit slips
through smoke-dense thatch
of the poet's darkened hut
touches the brewing cauldron
foments the brewing cauldron
of the dreamer's sleeping thoughts

pours in the stream
of sweet dark bounty
from the fairest of the trees
from the salmon's
willing flesh

hears the poet's gasp of insight
smiles
withdraws again

## Brigit's Candle Bearer*

acolyte's crimson face
reflecting Brigit's flame

splendid goldfinch
whistles in thistle stands

belly stroked in
pussy-willow hues

gleaming snowdrops
rime each cheek

rays of saint-tamed light
pierce folded wings

then cool in deepest shade
of earth black wells

# The Falcon*

so temperate
this faithful falcon
perched on your round and holy tower
chastely rebuffed all amorous advances
till the proper season when
in accordance with its nature
it made its way
to the mountains of Glendalough

far from the eyes and longings
of celibate monks and nuns
the falcon raised its family and returned
mate forsaken
to your tower once again

there it throve for centuries
venerated by townspeople
preying on perching bird and dabbling duck
loyal to you in some strange kind
long after you preceded it
from this earth

## Bear at Imbolc

bear sleeps

at Brigit's touch
awakens

womb of earth births
hungry bellies
for new-grown life to feed

## Woman in the Well

there is a wise woman in the well
her bones preserved for all of time
white root hairs    oak and beech
twine within her
she curls
in stone-scented darkness
our petitions fall like petals
as she sleeps

# Fionn and Brigit*

burial cairn at Almu
the place called Allen's Hill
slopes well known to Brigit

is it the tomb of Fionn
who quartered there?

landless warriors ran
with their Leinster hero
that seer basted with wise Salmon's
crisping oil
his thumb now a certain line
to Sight

he met the fearsome
fire-breather
slew it
made Tara safe

Fionn fair and Brig high
wisdom sparked in them
what encounters lost to us
did they share on sweet
Cill Dara's plains?

## Pillar   Stone   Fire

oak post   bold pillar rising
from fundament to sky
hearthfire snaps and sighs at your feet
smoke rolls in dull plumes upward
snatched through thatch-hole
cloaks you as you stand
in silent joining

two worlds you link

the poet smoulders   eyes closed
outstretched on feathered mantle
   swan necks   drake necks
reciting endless song
imbas awakens   ecstatic inspiration
lost in the currents of the Otherworld
she scales your heights

Brigit   bless roof-pole and ridge-beam
bless the well-fed hearth
be the stone on the poet's belly
the fire in his head

## Brigit Wakens

frost clutches the thorn
wrens huddle   feathers puffed
deer   stiff with cold
nip tips of willow twigs

Brigit wakens
kicks her feathered blanket from her legs
descends from her bed to the frozen lake

a touch of her palm
tames the water's tension
fingers melt its rigid plane
stir the cold broth mildly   back and forth

sleepy trout rise stipple-sided
from the muddy bed in sloth
spring smooths winter's transfixed edges
urges green and busy life
upon the land

## Brigit's Pastures*

bee releases the nuzzled
pale blue head of flax
hums heavy-bodied
rises legs dangling
zags across your plain

oak outspreads
long enduring limbs
in old contentment
your fox curled
sleeping at its feet

spring waters
earth cool   dark in flavour
crisscross the marshy ground
seep   to sunlight softly
whisper subtle blessings in your name

# Booleying Time*

she rests beside
their crooked hillside shelter
her sister's breath
past woven walls
whistles
softly in
softly out

darkness   mist

hooves heavy on soft earth
black shapes barely seen
mutter
now and then emit
low complaint

summer night is fresh

skin tingling
she sings
sings to you to keep them
well and safe
to lull her fears and keep her
well awake

no wolves tonight

cows grow fat on mountain flowers
hides sleeken
udders swell
and every day
butter for her to eat

far below
mother only now is resting
father close beside her
and brothers on the straw

*soon*
*little horned ones*
*we will go down to meet them*
*Brigit be your shield*
*from deer-pits and raiding men*
*falls from sudden cliffs*

*hush my darlings*
*don't worry*
*valley grass grows long*
*there'll be no repast of holly twigs*
*and fallen leaves*
*for you back home*

# Idyll

in the pool emerging
from your earth-clasped stream
three small white fishes describe
sacred paths
hazels drop ripe nuts into your waters
alder rise graceful from your banks
I plait the prayer I will leave for you
tied on a willow branch
each element of this silent place
you

## Numinous Land*

beneath the sun
golden wine-filled cup
giver of life
comfort to the dead
you dwell

every oak and thistle
every bog and stream
possessed of deities
you among them
seeping out
through cress and liverwort
stalking out on hoof and toe

standing here
I am drenched in divinity
this mist soaked land
these blue backed waves
this storm shocked
sun shattered sky

# Three Sisters at Drung Hill*
## (Charm at Lughnasa)

knees scour on rock
robes scrub thin
inch by inch we climb

do not avoid the pebble
do not shun
thorned twig

we climb
from foot of shore
to crown of hill

here well up
born of ember dropped
from uncharred skirt

pure sweet waters
(seen sometimes by chance
never found when sought)

glittering eyes dance
on skimming wet
we circle winking   smiling pool

celebrate harvest
cheer fallen corn
kiss fertile ground

on earth-rasped
deep devoted
heart sated

well enraptured
want-extinguished
knees

# Three Hags*

on her day the green things
think of growing

with the saint walking over them
the birds singing at sight of her
it's no surprise

so

under the soil
one hag
in veils like finest roots
is stretching sunward
pushing   pushing
the wee plants up

two hags with veils down-hanging
their wayward looks obscured
with double weight press
the dears back down

on Patrick's feast the weary one
wins over the second hag
together they push
and push

green shoots
fumble weakly for the sky

but sister three
scowling and besmirched
splays on her back above them

arms and legs out-thrusting
skirts    shawl sprawling over all

holds those plants hard down
beneath the earth

come the first of April
a turn of face
the three hags join together
no more contesting –
pressing    pleasing
grinning to themselves

and out the green things spring
into the light

# Brigit's Oaks*

your oaks
were the trees of my childhood

canopies of lobed leaves
crowned the streets of St James
sturdy scrapey-scratchy trunks and
crinkle-crankle limbs
their acorns fairy elegant
their fragrance woody and dense
their shade deep
on baking
prairie days

by late fall
only a few crabbed
yellow-ochre leaves still turned
on the lowermost branches
the street below
wore a crisp covering over soggy depths
leaves lay like saintly mantles
along curbs   on boulevards
through them I ploughed
kicking clods and clouds before me
of your dusk-scented vegetative earth

come Hallowe'en
all the neighbours clustered curbside
and right out on the street
grownups raked and shovelled mountains
of your leaves
mothers and children jacketed
thick-skinned potatoes in tinfoil

buried them in the depths
of those leafy mounds
flames were lit
bonfires grew
driving away the autumn chill
deep dark nutty smoke of oak
leaves and mast and fallen twigs
flames crackled   folk talked
darkness fell

later
– long   long later
it seemed to a waiting child –
carefully peeled charred foil
oak-roasted potato skins
gobs of margarine melting in
teeth softly pressed
through crumbling
sweetly scented flesh
most greatly favoured fruit
of the fertile earth

by Candlemas
cardinals wing-flashed
scarlet and black against the monochrome
your grey grooved trees stood
frozen   motionless
swathed in snow
deep drifts leaned against their flanks
and the long winter crawled steadily round
your waiting   watching   wondrous
sacred oaks

## Sunbeam

way off in the roiling furnace that is our sun
a ray of light shot out
sped
through the almost silent  almost empty
vacuum world of space
trained on infinity

it pierced a thin suspension of molecules
nitrogen  and something else
plunged  still frenetic
through kilometres of ever-concentrating air
came to a green wold in a pleasant
wooded land
where it entered by chance the open window
of a sacred dwelling house

and stopped
stunned
when a passing woman hung on it
her linen cloak

all that frazzled
frantic trembling energy
arrested
while Brigit wandered with a fellow saint
discussing God

## On the Burren*

on the deep-cleft Burren rocks
rain toils downward
pools in lightless caves
reaches ever down and down
seeps oil-dark to the sea

fragile blooms in wind-worn nooks
seabirds in their stone-borne nests
a pilgrim's leg might fracture
in some unregarded seam

they gather here to seek you
the injured and the ill
descend four steps to your cliff-well
few will spy you there

one year alone in seven
you appear
no longer than a finger
on each flank three ruddy spots
upon a blush of green
you emerge with friendly undulations
from beneath your roof of stone

the one who sees you
is three times seven blessed
cured of every ailment
in three short days

## Ancestral Dream

I lie beneath
the sprawling halo of the oak
its roots far sunk in the Otherworld
my eyes veiled and quiet
the tang of poetry light
upon my lips
and dream of you   Brigit

this dream
youngest daughter
of a thousand older dreams
your face transforms
in the changing light
voice to voice
silence to silence
so much forgotten
so much drawn anew

my ancestors lay
beneath the oak   the roof-pole
set out on journeys of the soul
their course   their vision
so different from my own

a goldfinch flutters in your
outspread arms above me
a gold-torced swan crests
the offering-pool
the sun-gold shimmer of your face
bends toward me   Brigit
golden scent of your amber honey
I breathe you in

with this dream of you I link hands
with those who came before me
where we would argue
where our hearts would meet
I cannot tell
but the warmth of imbas enters me
goddess of my kin
saint of my elder church
and through this dream of you
I rest with them

Poems – Hand

## Everywhere

Brigit! guess what!
I saw you at the market
bent over billiard-hard avocadoes
chin lifted slightly as you listened
to two young shaggy men
I saw the way you pierced
the truth of their existence
saw for myself the lick of fire emanating
from the younger's toque-clad forehead
the whitesmith's delicate hammer dangling
from the open fingers of the other's hand
you are everywhere!
even when I sag with rain and hunger
there you are
playing with light and darkness
carving depth
out of the commonplace

# One and Three*

Brigit
not meaning to pry but
can we face the point of your
triplicity?
triple goddesses
not rare among Celts
but see
these hold babies   nappies   basins
these bear gifts of fruit and flower

I don't dispute
your sovereignty over land
your protection of women birthing
your taste for healing   lactating ewes
       plentiful harvests of ale
but your tripleness seems
different to these others
your craft not only birthing
but metal   word  and medicine

how do you figure in?
how truly do you differ?
how can I best approach
one who is three
three who are one

three who are so unlike
those other
divine women
three?

# Multiplicity

a stone god stands on a forest path
two faces   peering forward
peering back
a goddess who is three
one sister guides the poet's fire
another steadies the smith
the third holds up the healer's craft

where can these not see
future   present   past
what distant aspect is not revealed
to the sisters three
the Brigits' piercing stare
in every direction
the realms encompassed
in their triple gaze

# Song of Brigit*

I am a currach riding deadly swells
strong   sure as a whale's back

rest with me

I am a brook smoothly winding
slitting earth and rock

drink of me

I am the sound of standing stones
the spear that halts destruction

endure with me

brandish me

who holds the flame within the pool?
who invokes the poet's spark?
who heals and fells with words?
forges sword and cauldron both?

I am the fullness of life
born of light   I wed the darkness

I am three   I am one
a wind-stripped cairn above the lake

know my mystery

stand with me

# Embody

I will not pray to you
not plead or explain
but live you out

this hand
holds the hammer
this brow
ablaze
this pool
scattered with healing herbs

where I was weak
I am bolstered
where I faltered
I am firm

my cauldron vast
and brimming
my judgement keen
my heart ready
for anything I meet

## Brigit in the Time Before

your land
curved and contoured
fleeced with trees
round each bend a place of magic
barrows   henges   raths
the land below won by your kin
the land above conceded
– with many breaches –
to the Gaels

salt butter in the souterrain
cheese upon the shelf
beef hung and rootstock in its place
your people bright in hill forts
in the white sun's gleam
before the others came

was it you who turned
the round stone quern
who shaped the gathered wool
who threaded warp through weighted weft
to weave the cloth
who drew the purple dye from lichen
red from alderbark
yellow from the many-blossomed weld

you who nursed the fosterchild
with chills and blistering ills
who wove the ancient songs by firelight

knot back your locks of gold
fair sister

fold back your sleeves of flax
your strong arms plunge
in fishing weir
and washing pool
your light laugh leaves its echo
on the bog

## Wolves and Pigs

there was a woman at that time in Ireland –

we didn't know then what would come
only what was
and it was good
woods wide and prosperous with deer and hare
vole-filled plains
even fine young calves left sometimes
exposed
away from the cloth-bound ones
the ones with cudgels and spears

we were many
joyous
families sprawled across loch-marked land
and we in every cranny
some even tasting the splendour of the sea

later the place itself would change
cloth-bound ones change and we would be
hunted to our last hard death
skins of our people sent across the waves

our hearts were wholly stopped
we dreamed and howled no more
among the night-dark hills and hollows

people came to ask
were there ever wolves in Ireland?

there were
and I was there

running with a pack more than twenty strong
twenty rich
uncles aunts and ungrown ones
our chiefs and all their children
guiding us in denning
guiding us in hunts
joining us in play
I was there
and those were blissful days

there was a woman then –
far from us but wolves have speech
we knew of her
heard her works
heard her plans
heard of the wolf she gentled
the dogs she fed
the harried boar she welcomed to her fold

so when the word went out of her intention
to send men on a walk of many days
to retrieve for her a gift of many pigs
we stepped out from the woodlands
skimmed up from the plains
circled down around the pig-man's hold
and drew his beasts as one

lean-meated  narrow-trunked  long-legged
rough-bristled creatures
we gathered them with pleasure
carefully
a pack knows best the art of driving
those who wish not be driven so

and so we did

a surging   moving   snorting mass
of sweet-hooved life
tight tails twisting protest
high voices squealing wrongs

none stood in our way
for we eschewed the tracks and roadways
led the swine through the home of trees
down stripling   wriggling streams that muddied at their step
we in silence flanking in the brush
until we met her party of men where the river finds the road

the pig-man knew them to be his own
his hale and hefty black-bodied brood
and gave them to her people
and when they turned to Leinster
sticks and calls and eager slapping hands
we withdrew away
the wild wolves who herded Brigit's pigs

# Contemplations

if I feel false
weaving together these
contemplations of my heart
when   O wise matron of the poet
will I feel true

if my praises are inadequate
my understanding small
my expression frail and weak
there is this
each moment I spend in struggle
to match words to your riches
is a moment when all else ceases
there is no past to reckon with
no future to organise
and I am gladly lost
alone with you

## Brigit Speaks with the Sword

Brigit steps on the field of heroes
red blossoms
black mud churned
lays a hand on every broken stem

knife cuts natal cord
scythe fells corn
sword harvests men

the smith prays to Brigit
grinds his blade sleek
hardens it as the warrior
shields his heart
but the goddess
is not numb to her tools

Brigit keens
addresses spell-rich sword

from earth we raised you
with fire made you
grieving and grateful
praise you
now help me   sword
dig furrows for our dead

# Invasions

Brigit of the Tuatha Dé Danann
they who mastered gods and demons
who ruled the island after many
and fell at last to Sons of Míl

Brigit saw the final battles
when the Tuatha fought the Gael

and her tribe defended bravely
but the Gaels pressed them down
slew them on the awful mountain
crushed them underneath the mound

so the Gael secured the bright lands
the Tuatha filled the lands below

with three races she had dealing
long before the Gael knew her
gave her honour   trust   devotion
even now she sees each world

how can we envision Brigit
what can we hope to ask of her

she who sees the Gael's essence
and the spirits in the landscape
Tuatha in the sacred places
Fomhoire hunched in shadow still

and the Fir Bolg long since vanished
all is carried in her heart

## At Battle's Pause*

the army turned for camp
trudged beneath weight
of bronze-bossed shields
long and broad enough
for a man to crouch behind
trudged beneath weight
of spear and sword
of thick-shafted javelin

beneath weight of bloody clothing
sagging   bitter wound
war-worn limbs
weight of handsome
gold-locked champion
once fierce   awhirl
in cutting   churning throngs
now still
and borne aloft

at your well  Brigit
they met their king
piled before him each a stone
and each a head
made of them a great cairn
upon the hero's form

healers gathered
brought their physic herbs
crushed and scattered them
till the water's anguished face
your precious healing pool
lay thick and green

in they dipped the injured
out soldiers sprang
renewed and hale

but even goddesses
must say farewell
to mighty dead

## Death of Goibniu's Grey

you know the smith god Goibniu
shout with him over clanging anvils
pour brimming metal into common moulds
share systems of enamelling
discuss together the right or wrong
of embossing thus
of spiralling thence
the fit moment at which to plunge
the fervid core into its watery berth

you knew his best-loved heifer
slender-horned and Otherworldly grey
Glas Goibniu of the placid disposition
darling of the smith's vast herd
and   ah
but she could let her milk come down

back then stars were scarce in the darkness
illuming night but palely
without the full moon's aid

a woman of malice
envy and spite
sidled up to Goibniu night and day to sneer
that poor sad cow of yours
she's no great milker
she's no so grand
I've a vessel she could never fill
and Goibniu in his folly
swallowed her bait

so it was to your dismay   Brigit

protector of herds   mother of smiths
you saw the cullender placed beneath
Glas Goibniu's teats
watched the milk fall from her
course through the much-pierced bowl
till even the black sky above
was streaked with white
and Goibniu was without
his queen of cows

## Sovereign Goddess

my people     my tribe
busy in their industry
ready with their laughter and their arms

my creatures
hidden and bold
hunted and left to be
mares and foxes
wolves and cows

my cornfields   my berries
vast peatbogs of offerings
butter
gold
wood
and the mast-filled
fuel-filled
strength-filled forests
that grace my frame

you   stranger   look at me
with eyes of greed
eyes that do not see
my waters
feeding   cleaning
reviving those who fall
my ridges and my cairns
each holds a standing warrior

you do not see the king who weds me
his beauty unsurpassed
justice and honour his two arms

truth and danger his two legs
you do not see my druids   my poets and artisans
their combined arts shall bring your people down

you do not see my women
you do not see my men
you do not see the girdle of the sea
that binds them to me
the blanket of the sky that holds them here
you do not see

go
and the brain your head contains will remain there
your breast will continue unspeared
you will not feel the shock of my reaction
– my very stones will be turned against you –
if you act on what you're thinking

stranger with eyes of greed

## Verb: Smith

smith equals verb
there is no noun about it
tie on black scarred
leather apron
heft each tool
file crud
smooth
anvil
peer into
fire

feed fire
damp fire
control

fire

no weak arm this
wrapping fingers firm
around an iron shaft
then dive into pit of fiery hell
see blood red then apple red
then blazing orange
slide the shaft out from the pit

and wield the hammer
thunder blows
one and one and one
again again against the yielding shaft
and there
fine movements
flick this way  turn that

black-orange rod becomes
thing of grace

## Goddess of Smiths

breath dissolving iron
liquid bronze and gold
white heat who destroys
with one cruel blow
you guide the hammer   Brigit
death and life together
forging to shatter
shattering to forge anew

and what is fashioned

cookpot for the hospitaller
vast enough to hold a cow
ale crock   chariot furnishing
offering dish   cloak pin
sword

beat me on your anvil   Brigit
melt me in your pot
knit me solid
make me whole
bring from me a fine bossed cauldron
offering to your endless round

in this life and the next
this life and the next

# Bres the Beautiful

i/

of Eochaid Bres it was said
every thing of beauty in Ireland –
plain and fortress   ale and candle
woman   man   and horse –
will be judged in relation to that boy

ii/

when the king weds the land
she flourishes

king to goddess
father-god to mother-land
truth to bounty

when his rule is just and generous
people   plantings   beasts
fruits of forest
fruits of labour
bloom

he who breaks this unity
shatters all

beware the king who pinches back
envies and holds down
his child will die
goddess-land will howl
in wrath from him recoil

though he scheme and bargain
he is lost

iii/

this is how I heard it told
let it not be so

if not for Bres
the first battle of Mag Tuired
would have been the last

if not for him
accord between two peoples
ties already forged
would not firmer bind
art with husbandry
light with dark

if not for him
your child would not have lived
would not have died
you would not have raised
like a sword on which to fall
the keen in Ireland

if not for him
no satire in the land
and too – remember this –
no secrets of field and corn

your husband   Brig
beautiful   beloved
bent within
as a poor-smithed nail

iv/

when the battle was lost to the Tuatha
they closed on Bres to kill
he bargained for his life:
the cows of Ireland will always
be in milk

this did not suffice

the fields of Ireland will bear harvest
every season of the year

this did not suffice

they asked instead
tell us how to plow
how to reap and how to sow
if you tell us this
you will be saved

so he told them the way
he told them the day
on Tuesday plow
on Tuesday sow
on Tuesday reap

and he was spared

v/

Bres  in situ
threshold god
wed to threshold goddess
farmer god
wed to wild land

sunlight
your mother
seafoam
fathered you

beautiful horseman
before the scribal edits
before the changing
fortunes of your land

you shone

# Ridge of Clay*

nine women
Brigit at their head

twist wattles through
bowing hazel withes
knot ropes
smear dung and mud
on their inaugural hut
by the oakwood that endures
upon the Ridge of Clay

she says

this will be Cill Dara
Cell of the Oak
most exalted tree
most carved of craftsmanship
that splendid river coursing
we shall call Amhain Líffé

we will dig the clay
of this strong ridge
build our community
God's rib-bone mined by
Adam's ribs

(nine smile
the tenth  is grinning back
such the heady brew
of their work)

we will build ourselves
a house of worship
build ourselves
a vibrant home

oaks will always grow
in wise profusion
cattle walk the Curragh
in common pasturage

and when this
our first hut
is raised up

we will plant our seeds
and tend the soil
that we have come to claim

# Three Brigs and Sencha*

i/
the judge   Sencha
founder of the lore
conceiver of the law

before him
chaos
before him
a world ungoverned

even he might err

he judged poorly
the inheritance of woman
on his face in true fashion
blisters boiled

but Brig of the Judgements
with her words made it right

of all the texts of Irish law
of all their many judgements
equal to all the feathers of every fowl
only this they say
was made by woman

false proof now sound
daughters rightly protected
fruits of woman's work
ownership of land

blemish gone

ii/
who was this Brig?
only his child

who was his wife?
also Brig

who his mother?
Brig as well

Brig of the Cowless
Brig of the Judgements
Brig of Hospitality
father of lore   this Sencha
and
son
husband
father
of wise
wise Brig

## Blessing Against Oppression and Submission

you who ran unconstrained
across the Curragh
stand between me and slavery

as you shattered the lies
of the shrewd
would-be rapist
would-be owner of his
intended thrall
freed his victim
now sovereign again
over
spirit   body   heart

bless me
protector of women and the bound

you knew your path
though yourself a slave
made them set you free

set me free

enquired of the mute child
what do you want?
though others cried   impossible!
did not stir until
she found and made her choice

let me know the truth
of my own thoughts
the liberty to follow them

where I must

bless     preserve
enlighten me

long against danger
give me aid

# Cormac's Gift

picture Cormac
still a youthful monk
not yet bishop
nor yet king
nor yet saint whose relics
produce omens
miracles

clothed in rough linen
feet wound with skins
packed with straw
to keep them warm

sickle in one calloused hand
he cuts galls from oaks
scrapes bark from ash trees
over slow flames simmers them
in white sharp wine

boils and cools
boils and cools

blends in sticky
light-snaring
gold acacia gum
jay-wing blue crystals
of Roman vitriol
sets the mess aside
tightly capped
to rest

files his metal pen

to a perfect point

Cormac writes
so they say
leans over roll of
well tanned calf
and steady
writes his glossary
the stem of every L
the arms of every T
each bite of his acid
brown-black oak-gall ink
sinks deep

here
like dandelion seed
to ripen and to burst
lines of you
learned woman
daughter of the Dagda
with his cauldron and his club
poets worshipped you
your superintendence
noble    great

and more
two sisters besides
both named Brigit
woman of healing
patron of smiths
with all the Irish
Brigit was called
goddess

these are serious words
serious
and nearly lost

if not for Cormac
his steady labours
a thousand years ago
alone amid the silent pens

for none had etched
your name in stone
no queen bore your title
no stories of you were
whispered round the fire

if you were     goddess
if    indeed    you were
we would not know
you would be a ghost    a guess
a glimmer
behind the blaze
of the saint

# Pillars of the World*

two pillars of the world
Patrick and Brigit together

(as the pillars of the ancestors
once stood
creating worlds
sustaining them
till the sky should fall
and all its stars upon our heads
the earth shatter
the sea emerge
a shroud
to sweep us to our deaths)

# Indictment and Defense*

Patrick   they say
shooed snakes from Irish soil
with mighty hands pulled down
the pagan tent
deities demoted
beings of leaf and horn
chased
to the limits of the world

you too
saint of Leinster
must shoulder blame

*sister   you are right*
*yet when Patrick ground his axe*
*and tugged at tents*
*did I not leave the ridgepole standing*
*some glamour in the gaze*
*let immortals glimmer through*
*in certain light*

## To Alba

Brigit came

on Uist
well-gnawed bed of Hebridean rock
she blessed the oyster-catcher
in her nest of speckled eggs
steadied birthing women on shaking knees
faced fierce winds of every sort
wings of angels beating at her back
knew
her people and her God with stubborn love

came Colum Cille

on another rock he built his bed of stone
high above the pleasant green he groaned
God   let my sufferings bear fruit
and fruits beyond imagining they bore

saints of Ireland

sea gladly carried them
new lands claimed them
gathered in tight embrace
came to cherish   need   depend

strangers from a land of risk
fragile sailors in frisking
oarless boats

Brigit and Colum Cille no longer
now Bride and Columba

## The Community Learns to Read

outside the small tightly-wattled hut
roof thatch straight and neatly trimmed
your virgins settle on their skirts
gather round the new-come book

one and then another of you
traces stout letters
moves lips
a glitter in the eye as words take shape

what delight to you
to each of them as well
as these now familiar concepts
awaken beneath your questing eyes

one day
when you are fluent in this work
you will steep your eyes again
in godly words

a young girl will sit behind you
watching every movement
as you lift your pen
and drench it with your ink

## Old Shawly

nods and grins
sorts carrots into piles
tucks the grey shawl
into her puckered skirt waist

hair enclosed in that old kerchief
like her sisters and their sisters and
all the old shawlies in the village square
fish wives   sellers of old clothes
one who stands and wobbles
and this one with her pipe

she has walked since dark to be here
you have just risen from your bed
haggle over the pittance
that she asks

old shawly nods and grins
says yesh mishus
folds carrots in old newsprint
takes what you offer

she has sewn inside her skirt
a hidden pocket
two pound notes   a shell
Saint Brigit pressed onto
a piece of tin

says Blesh you mishus
tucks your pennies
in her pocket
when you go

# Healing Goddess

she heals

her sisters compose weapons of war
weapons of fiery brow
sword and word equal in their blow

she heals

dip
the injured fighter in her pool
pack his wounds with herbs
sing soft the pain that racks him

another warrior fit for battlefield

and once again
sister Brigit heals

# Stand Strong

may I be filled with loyal friendship
for the land and every being that she bears

may I remain pledged
to the welfare of my people

through trust and determined application
may I ignite with poetry   strike wisdom
from the daily flint

may I forge a worthy foundation
lustrous and true

may I heal what is sick
make whole what has broken

for the goddess who offers us her body
who holds us that we may be and grow
does so for the benefit of the tribe
ours and hers

she supplies us many tools
carves out many paths

may I accept her gifts with gratitude

I swear by the gods my people swear by
I will stand strong

# Shattered Dreams

you can heat the brand too long
rain too many blows
bend the iron far too many times

dreams shatter
no longer iron rods but brittle glass

no healer lives who has not closed
eyes glazed at last

no poet who has not failed to find
the blaze he sought

look
the corners of the smithy
stacked iron
cold    rust-chewed
abandoned things

there is no chill like the forge
when the blacksmith downs her tools

when the time to strike
the time to tend
the time to pen is past
draw my breath into your bellows
feed your forge anew

let me be dissolved
resolved
made other   made whole
made true

## Held

I lay my head against your naked breast
ah   soul
I am at rest

do not stir
breathe                 only breathe
your warm skin is my perfect bed

how many years since I have rested so?
breathe   Mother       only breathe
consolation I thought I could not know

sleep eludes me
life eludes me
I am shattered to my core

and here you are

I lay my cheek against your naked breast
I do not stir
I do not sleep

I rest
ah   my soul
I rest

# The Briugu

at Brigit's guest house

the knock of nail in board
the cough of tiller in earth
the lace of new leaves
lifting from pungent soil
the whisper of winnowed chaff
the scent of bracken beer
the roll of long-handled spoon
in well-stocked vat
the pluck of poet's harp
the shout of smith's iron
the mewl of calf
for his mother's teat
the press of feet to river
the impression of knees at well
the throat-song of warblers
the scratch of dogs in midden
the bite of needle in wool
the trespass of breeze through
unshuttered doorways
the rustle of pen on skin
the voice of man lent in surety
against another's debts
the grunts of foster children
at their game

the sudden laugh
of welcomed traveller
at Brigit's house

## Womb Blessing

Brigit may your fertile well
heal my empty womb
children to cheer me
to work beside me
to carry me
when I fall back
to your earth

# Your Feast is Upon Us*

tender fish and young onions
the last of last year's corn
the first of this year's milk
and the eye of the sun
warm on wood and field

a blessing to be so cared for
fed till the last mouth sated
each growling belly full
sweet ale to soothe and cheer us
in friendship and in thanks

# Hearthfire

this morning I rise and waken
the sleeping flame of my hearth

Brigit of the blessings
kindle me
let me burn off self-deception
extend protective warmth to all
to friend and foe   to hawk and hen
to those who worry or repel
let me build a fire of choicest fuels
to withstand the dousing waters
of my fear

when I lie down tonight
hearthfire banked
red-gold marrow beneath
the soft grey mantle of its ash
lie with me   Brigit
your flame enfolding mine
burning low and gentle
till sunlight breaks the dark

## Fisherman's Shield

sleep yet dully gnawing
he wakens
burrows up through dark

whispering to herself
she too draws up
from black to black

she lights a candle
he slides into his sweater
knit in calligraphic paths
blessed by dew on Brigit's Eve
as the saint passed by

straightens it round himself
cold wool on warm underclothes
their home's best prayer
entwines him now

into the darkness steps

she hears his feet
on stones along the path
he crunches down
to join the waiting sea

## A Blessing on Your Nets*

tiny turbaned winkle
shrinking like a mouse
me and all my brothers
in corners of your house
a blessing on your nets
we bring
we wither and we die
a blessing on your nets
we bring
but we'll not cry

# Healing Ways*

bath of herbs    bath of milk
porridge of oats and hazel buds
and tender meadow leaves
these are the ways of healing

saffron when spirit's low
cupping quells bones aflame
butter coaxes thorns
from flesh

sweat house
icy pools
rubbing limbs
these grow forceful
the lagging frame

lost in prayer you dimpled
the stones beneath your knees
where water pools today
cures joints and livid eyes
women with child
kneel there
and birth is kind

ways of healing   many
prescription always the same
place yourself in the hands of the land
trust your soul to the saint

## Birth Blessing

your brat to shield my womanhood
your well to make me bloom
your girdle to ease my burden
  keep me safe
your mantle to lighten my labours
when the final hours are come
and bring my willing
worried breasts to leak

## History of Pain in Ireland

I've a stiff neck and bad teeth
like my people before me
blame the soil
blame the toil
Brigit   hear my plea

## Keeper of Cattle*

Brigit   divine cowherd
keep us from straying
save us from harm

tend your rumbling
wayward herd
lead us to sloping summer meadows
watch over us beneath the high sun
bring us home again
when nights grow long

your mother's companions
bathed you in milk at your birth
the red-eared cow of the Otherworld
became your only nurse

nine times the butter churned by you
nine times the flow from your milker's teats
the pail resounds
with your cascading gift

divine maid of the dairy
coaxing milk
from the skittish heifer with your song
you offer her first droplets to the sídhe
trace her flank with the cross of Christ
sooth the bawling
orphaned calf with gentle touch

sing sweet encouragement   Brigit
that we may overflow with offerings
that we may low in good contentment
sheltered together in you

## By Brigit's Day*

milk retreats to the cow's horns
from Christmas to Imbolc –
with your return
the cow gives milk again

wild birds mate
jackdaw and grey crow
the hen's egg   brooded
hatches safe and strong

nothing in water
or on the ground
is not thinking of propagation

the farmer knows it

if he has not written his name
on the land by Brigit's day –

his work is late

# Cattle in Winter*

we see you in our sunny summer thoughts
with tidey swaying kine
bellies wide
udders swinging
teat-tips milky    pink
their broad splayed hair-fringed toes
your strong bent dusty ones
clinging to the pebbly path as together
you climb the crooked hill

but what of spring
not gauzy blooming spring but shrill crisp
wintery spring
when cattle carved to a rickle
of skin and stabbing bone
so faint from hunger they must be
lifted to their feet
– new grass just peeping tender
from the earth –
are nicked with the knife
on the tail a few joints down
poultice of precious garlic and butter
firm tied upon the cut

with your aid and blessing
with the girding of the poultice
with the help of strong arms   steadying hands
they might come round
might nibble at the greenshoots
live to low and calve another time

so – that cow we see you with
visiting our dwellings late on Brigit's Night
sleek     fat     red ears twitching
she is something special
someone quite divine
someone stepping from the place where victuals
never fail
no ordinary starving human cow

# Bealtaine Cattle Blessing*

three drops in the cow's right ear
from the muddy   blessed pool
three drops in her nostril
and three in her pink mouth
she'll be good and steady for the year

who is it gives such blessings
is it Saint Finbarr   is it Brendan then

I think that it is Brigit
patron of the cattle   saint of the dairy too
she who went over and above the limits of charity
even her master loved her
and blessed her on her way
who but Brigit would set aside this pilgrim's place
for the people and their sick and suffering kine

## Milk, A List*

milk
the prime fruit of cattle (after butter)
(rare the day that meat is on the plate)

in winter milk retreats to the cow's horns
Imbolc – the time of milking

infant Brigit bathed in milk at birth

cure for poison
bathe in the milk of one hundred and fifty
white
hornless
cows

# Wielder of the Sword

I don't crave that meeting
with your sweetly crafted blade
head from body   severed
I roll apart
whatever bit of me escapes in one last sigh
sublimed
no time for final thought

nor do I wholly fear it

life will always seem too short to me
but broad like mountain pasture
it has been
each step as if on different qualities of soil
each rock's voice unique
each glimpse of each familiar thing
however often seen
unlike each time before

again   yet new

I once yearned to ride your chariot
headlong through the world
so many dreams to set in motion
so much to learn   to see   to do
now a junco scratching
for birdseed in the leaf-fall
is more than I could ever hope
to know

don't hurry to take me
sacred swordsmith

postpone the need to roll your sleeves
deliver the final blow
but when it comes
if I cringe in raw reflexive terror
smile for me
long enough that I can see you
then let me go

# Three to One

the triple pipes played
three clear melodies
each distinct
for three divine sisters
sword
herb
and song

one tune now
supplants the three
when we call
which sister hears
who considers
who responds

a thousand blurring years
deletions   foldings in

yet your eyes still startle
your voice inspires
you whisper in the waters
crackle in the flames

and the heavy horned cattle
the fox in the greenlit hedge
the red-billed shorebird scurrying
across the stony beach
know your stories
and sing your name

## Ogam Reading*

in the ogam I have drawn
two feda flank me
Dair on the left   Lus on the right
two branches of Brigit
your oak   knotted and grey
your flame and healing herb

two more feda
Gort   the garden   signals
some burgeoning in my life
Onn   wheel and fundament
cautions
build a firm foundation
from which to move

these four ogam together
surround me as an ancient
sacred grove
and a smooth stable chariot
prepared for flight

# Poems – Heart

# Invitation

come visit me Brigit
the cat will yield you the comfy chair
raise his head for your benediction
I'll pour hot bubbling water over mint
pull back the curtains   slide open the door
let in the cool garden air to refresh you
you can be yourself
goddess   saint   or some unexpectedly
ordinary woman   with tired hands
with chipped and missing teeth
we can muse together over the demands
of tending a hearth in modern times
you can have my bed
I'll sleep on the camping mat
there's so much I'd love to learn from you
how it all unfolded   how it looks to you now
or we could just be quiet
enjoying the night
and the sound of distant cars
on the rain-wet road

## Mother of the Saint

think of her
there amid the cows
their heavy udders swinging
she singing
singing though she had
endless work to do

and you
tiny at her feet crawling round
the ground cool and pleasant
the cow-earth soft and warm
a happy place to crawl

until her call
she lifts you by the armpits
dips you in the running stream
unseen
the love she bears yet solid
in her arms

charms
they say that you had miracles
from the moment you saw birth
yet no power to keep Broicseach
at your side

no surprise
you felt passion for the poor
the bonded   stolen
impressed
blessed

west those many miles you went
to find her
finally held her
mother child and mother
once again

## Convert

raised by druid
nursed by Otherworldly cow
you swore by the gods
your people swore by
every deity real in their eyes

(and you free to follow any cult
honour any deity when need arose)

this newcomer whose disciples
snubbed the ones who had shaped
had held your world so long

was it love of a Christian foster-mother
fear of choosing wrong
dread of yet more sorrow in your unfree life

or was it a quiet growing certainty
that this Christ
one of so many
was the god for you

did you tell the sun of your decision
the sacred grove   the red-eared deer
did you whisper to the waters
of your well

did the elements embrace you
as you stepped upon your Christian path
did you ever look behind you
and regret

# A Woman with God*

see her Brigit

there she walks

no land   no wits
no power to amuse

wanders tribal lands
eats cress with muddy fingers

from circling pools
grabs at darting minnows

like the doe
is dumb

milk for her
a salted loaf

he who gives her drinks
who urges her to steal

who gives to her
a belly big with child

he is the one
the law frowns upon

the people bear the cost of her
unprotesting

for she wears the mantle
of her God

good Brigit

when the woman crosses the Curragh
shambles through your house

you go to her with fine meat
oaten cakes

honey
to bring her smile

## Dubthach Versus the Druid*

much is made of your father
Dubthach
how you lived with him and worked
in his dairy
how you gave away his splendid things
his gold   his sword
his butter and meat

but what of the druid
who bought from him
your pregnant mother

your birth on his threshold
his care as you grew

was he not the true father
of your childish heart

did not his love of gods
obedience to sun and earth
his store of lore and genealogy

shape your vision of your world
give you perfect apprehension
of this sacred pagan place

if in time you drank
from another cup
where a Son
predominates

were you not still at ease
in flesh and heart
among the spirits
of land and beasts

so the oaks embrace you
you know the fox's speech
the snowdrop lifts its head
where you have trod

in you they recognise
the blood of one
who lives upon the limen
walks in bright accord
with sanctity

# Brigit and Her Sisters

were you there
hidden in the mild
child-embracing Virgin
in female saints and martyrs
who rose like lurid flames
from holy cards and soaring
self-sacrificing tales
in nuns who swept in grand
black gowns and spotless wimples
rosaries big as dog-ropes
swinging from their waists
down streets in twos and threes
into church for mass
into class
rolling impossible sleeves
dashing straight lines
perfect circles
with their well-aimed chalk
writing in elegant copperplate
*Sister* –
followed by their names in Christ

was that you
smiling out from behind raspberry red
ointment dabbed coaxingly
painlessly against my twitching
bloody knee
you and your two sisters
cloistered in tiny
fantastic rooms above the church
tossing balls for loping alsatians
scrubbing floors to high polish

tending ailing elders
teaching us to pray for pagan babies
promising to come back when you died
and describe heaven
so we wouldn't have to wait

you may have been grumpy
bossy even sometimes
but you were always down there
on your knees with the rest of us
labouring to make
to do  to understand  to serve
to be as good as we could be
not remote in thunderous heavens
sermonising on a mount
smashing tables in some merchants'
lending place

is that how I came to never quite relinquish
all that love and trust
that wish for sanctity

when God and his minions judged
and found me badly wanting
you embraced me although I'd run away
gave me cookies and grownup tea
let me know however bad I was
I was always good

# Appeasement*

on the Eve of Bride
we wove your cradle
your figure out of oats
called *welcome*
as you walked
the eyeless night

come Bride
welcome   stop with us

we offered food and rite
in your holy name
made place for you
at our ample board

come Bride
welcome   stop with us

best fed in all of winter
well content
hopeful you had heard
our ardent prayers

we levelled the ash
smoothed the ash
in the sleeping hearth
awaiting the sign
that you had been
had blessed

come Bride
welcome   stop with us

morning shatters

no print of heel
no mark of saintly sole
left in the still warm ash
no dent from the tip
of your slender
white birch staff

come Bride
we beg you   stop with us

how did we fail you
beauteous Bride
how did we disappoint
in shame and fear we made
your sacrifice

come Bride
we beg you   stop with us

dug a hole where
three cold streams
braid whispering to one
pressed in the twisting
fertile fowl

come Bride
we beg you   stop with us

spaded on the stony earth
covered for you
this bird not black nor white
not living nor yet dead

nor in the world nor in
the place below

come Bride
we beg you   stop with us

mother of the threshold
have mercy on us
those whose need is stark
whose hearts are true

come Bride
welcome   stop with us

take this gift
we beseech you
be forgiving

come Bride
welcome

bless our home

## Your People

on a windstruck island
your people dwell
Plain of Delight   Land of Ever Young
sun glints
rises from mist and salt's embrace
(mounds of gravel
barges of crushed and banded cars)

under bogs of feathered peat
red and green and gold
in rush-fringed black-watered
inland lakes
cached with shattered
(there was a story of a fine horse)
unused bronze and plain-carved wood
deep in the barrow hill
time unhinged
space irrelevant
they live

gods become fairies

short-lived
time-bound
men in caps
women in shawls
work land   harrow sea
fear the fairies'
jealousy and greed
come to see you
Brigit
as their own non-god

powers over theirs
(above us   Father over all)
born of the same earth
kneeling on the same stone
praising the same Name

you of all gods endure
        in their minds
        on the soft face of the land
(in the old church
they build a stage
coffee steeps
wifi
poetry)

## Famine Years

how you wept  Brigit
when potatoes blackened
turned to muck
your people driven
starving from their homes

when   hollowed
hewn
they gave their bodies for a meal
chewed grass
bled the landlord's cattle
sank
bone and skin
into the bog

they carried you
in their names
their hearts
their cries and whispered prayers

those who could
fled your land of new leaves
and whispering rain
their passage paid on rotting ships
promised food and money
given none
carried you to Grosse Isle and New York

those with some small
plot of tillage
stood guard against the starving
over the last unblighted earth

and workhouse yards gaped
with common graves

how bitterly it struck you
that your children suffered so
you knelt beside them as they died
in Irish hedges
or massed in reeking holds
or yellowed   gaunt   crawling overground
spurned by those who feared the fever
on some longed-for distant shore

## Walk of the Brigidines*

where else but here
do Christian and Neo-Pagan
flow so merrily together

Lá Fhéile Bríde – St. Brigit's Day –
when blame suspends
suspicion halts

holding high your flame

singing

justice

honour

tranquility

a river of lovers

snakes through

your holy sites

# Forgotten Saint

she was a short woman
heavy hair the colour of peat
plaited    pinned back recklessly
her skin a swarthy caste
hips    hands    forehead
broad and strong as rock

she never read
nor spoke from a pulpit
and no
she didn't appoint bishops
hang her garment on a beam of sun
cause milk to flow
from calfless teats

she never met Saint Patrick
didn't catch the slippery Christ
squeezed from his mother's pelvis
never was a goddess
though she believed in many
– her God was well accompanied

the land spoke to her
birds' pathways meant much
a poem sung on an injured part
could heal

Yeats would not have known her
we would not have known her
she would have stared at us
from crooked brows
if she had seen how we picture her

would have trod on
momentarily
a sort of prayer inherent
in her breath    her step
her glance at the harebell
on the moist edge of the spring

## Ordination of Brigit, Bishop*

your fingers
careless
light as lacewings
glance off my hardened heartwood
long dead altar in this
dark church

green blushes
forgotten channels rush
with wakened life
leaftips lift upward
branchlets purl out
from my curtained board

priest speaks quickly
words not under his control

as you are raised
from simple nun to bishop
you raise me in my turn
from lifeless slab
to teeming wood

## Nonbeliever

I do not believe in anything
in Goddess   God   or Fairy
in Angel   Demon  or Saint
I believe in nothing
(white sun pulsing in red wheat)
my heart opens like a field to rain
when I sense your touch

# First Encounter

picture the seeker
young or steeped in age
fingers fast on keyboard
or happy touching
pages of a book

her thoughts arrested
his heart
speeding up a little bit

this Brigit
something of her speaks to me
anvil and forge
green-leafed healing
liquid poetry
a goddess who is many
yet is one

there is something here that draws me
well of clooties and of prayers
a fire always tended
never dies

and she is pulled to know you
he is called to learn your name

## Conversation in Queen's Park

when we first met I circled round you
taking note
this is how you differ from the
One True God I had been schooled to
this is how you fit into
the same garment that he wore
wary  I wondered at your gentleness
the marvel of your womanly profile
familiar saintly odour
new sharp fragrance of goddess strength
and nowhere a gavel forcing agreement
where none exists

you gave me room to breathe
I learned what I could of you
wove your images into me
dyed with you the patterns of my life
sunrise and sunfall
winter and spring

soon I came to you
with petitions and with prayers
please protect us
please stop the hurt
please give me strength

I found sisterhood in you
your daughters coming to my table
we prayed together and built our lives

then it came to me to give you thanks
for all that was   all that had been

and all that never came to be
to offer praise and gratitude
for everything

stranger
mother
sister
friend
our time together grew long

I sit now beside you
on an old park bench
this stone could be an altar
this park
a sacred grove
you are a weathered and timeless woman
your brown dog waddles elderly off its leash
I see you now and there is only silence
nothing to offer   ask   or say
like I am an ancient hazel tree
and you my silent wife

# Initiation

I pledged myself to you
one Imbolc long ago
in a steep
and hidden wood

stepped from
my old dress
sank in your
ice-fed
furling stream
bare limbs motionless
head submerged
in throttling
Otherworldy flow

shock of you
stripped breath
thought
time

I emerged flame-headed
up moss-slick rocks

new robe awaited
but no cold
could overtake

laughed
wet and naked
among your trees

# Brigit Three (Offering Prayer)

Brigit Three
Goddess of smithing
Goddess of healing
Goddess of poetry

I ask for your presence
listen if you will
accept my offering
hear my plea

great are you
worshipped by craftsmen
bestower of skills
source of the keenest spark

fire in your Forge
fire in your Well
fire burning in the Head

I bring you the ogam
Tinne for Smith
nGétal for Healer
Lus for Poet
strong letters
filled with wisdom
I honour you with them

these I offer
fine tool of iron
roots and stems of healing
song that I sing for you

I ask your aid
guidance   protection
sweet inspiration
enfold me   surround me
comfort me Brigit

this I ask
a home I delight in
health and discernment
good work and good family

Brigit Three
Goddess of smithing
Goddess of healing
Goddess of poetry

I give you thanks
I give you thanks
I give you thanks

## – I'm Asleep and Don't Waken Me – *

there's a bright-headed woman
overlooking my bed
– I'm asleep and don't waken me –
with burgeoning hair
like a poolside of cress
– I'm asleep and don't waken me –
she won't lift a finger
to dim my dream
– I'm asleep and don't waken me –
but stands till I rise
as the white-minnowed spring
– I'm asleep and don't waken me –

## Brigit's Hermit

these mornings are joy
making clean
keeping well
this one room and all that dwells
stray cat
blinking at my door
slip of soap and strength of water
strength of hands wringing cloth

I have a gift
silent living
twined with sacred song and dharma talks
all reminding of the cheer of this pure
pleasant duty

I wrote once of a lover
a mother and a friend
the shape of my world
was uncertain then
this is who I have become
a monk              ordained by self
who keeps her hermitage
who steps into the world
and when it's time
returns
opens window
opens door
the air is gentle and on it come
small and lovely friends
moth   mosquito   singing wasp
across the threshold step
silk-limbed spiders

and here is wood bug
here is silverfish

if I am too old
as I always was too grumpy
to meld with a community of nuns
I am not too old
and never too grim
to make a sweet cell of my home
a bird's nest living in my heart

## Four Corners to My Bed*

*On Lying Down*

i/
four corners to my bed
Brigits three and Eochaid Bres
guarding head and heart and hand
hearth and harvest
spring and land

ii/
I stretch myself across my bed
as Brigit stretched her mantle

starting modest
sweeping vast

taking only
and entirely
what we need

*On Waking*

four corners when I rise
all made pure
error     illusion     lies
every failing that we share
rising
        rising
clearest eye
begin again
                rising
sun and air

# Praise Song

I sing praise praise praise
many times upon this hill

sing thanks for my release
into this world

splendid
unstruck note

each stem and seedpod
trill and cry
reflects one tiny aspect
of your song

I sing thanks thanks thanks
many times upon this hill

sing joy of seeking
though I do not behold

beholding
though I do not see

seeing
though I do not comprehend

sing praise praise praise
and thanks

## Prayer for the Dead

dear Brigit
I lay my loved one down
a last time

he is three days dead
we have wailed and wept
we have sung and laughed
we have given thanks
we have cried out in anger

we have given thanks

bless my loved one on his journey
let his coracle be light and leaping
on the waves

salmon his companions
and the great whales
to guide him to his home

# Pause

why fear death?
no heaven and hell for me
the spirit released
finds its way again
my final breath
just a pause in one long life

beside my corpse
a pen please –
carved feather of a swan –
and a taper of honey wax
to guide me from where
my spirit roams
home again to you

## Brigit to the Grieving Mother

my sister
you have tasted bitter herbs
she who you loved sleeps
dead upon your breast
as he who I loved
slept on mine
the whole world knows this torment
the whole world sorrows
with your woe

hold your daughter
till the knife's edge blunts
bring her to me
her soft limp form
place gently in my hands

go to your people
rebuild your house
let the wounds upon you bleed
until they seal

I will hold her in her sleeping
I will take her to my hidden well
some day
this tiny soul
will live anew

# Hard

i/
if only you'd been there
instead of endless
icy driving
hard
silent light
high windows

fear
shame
hope

keep it   she advised
give it away
(harsh now) drive to the states
make the father pay

hard looks
harder choices

ii/
before I woke
embalmed in sorrow
this molten keen and I
forever one

nurse shakes me
stark room
hisses
you're disturbing
the other patients
(with my grief)

iii/
if only I had been
not me
childlike    destitute
but instead
that lucky nun

your hand on my belly
pity in your eyes
my sweet child
quietly withdrawn

kind
soft
comforting

safe
healed
whole

## Prayer with Cancer

dear gentle Bridie
come this quiet night
a hole is burned in me
I ask your help

come on silent feet
silent as cancer grows
Imbolc to Midwinter
seen   unrecognised

I am hot wax melting
sorrow at this threat
to precious life
fear trickles   cool
at its back

midwife to Mary
matron of the healers
of the Sídhe
bright butter bearer
blessed mantle wearer

teach me
body heart and mind
to live
to die
to be

## The Blessing I Ask

we've come to you
for every kind of blessing
on house
on love
on health
all your people have drawn
to your golden radiant flame
from dangers winged and clawed
from mysteries dumb

I don't fear the eagle and fox
the restless great-hipped bear
my water is clean
my cupboard middling full

but blades churn
I am harrowed
if the grave was close around me
I couldn't be more bound

this ancient shadow
steals my breath
this fire leaps and jerks
this hammer madly
clamours at my chest

here is the blessing I ask Brigit
forget I asked the rest

ease the breath that feeds me
bless and ease my fear
ease and bless the rage

that scalds and scrapes

haul me in your chariot
keep me a time with you
help me tame this striving
saddened beast

remind me of the marigold
chin turned to perfect sun
the pure birch standing
flakes of gold on slender bone
in that sun's light

show me the bending hill
your strong   raised knee
the scented pool
cradled in your palm

and I will remember
I will again remember
joy hidden
just beneath my fear

## That I May Share

I make this offering
of ale and of butter
of my own supper   halved
that I may learn to give
that I may offer wealth
that I may share nourishment
that I may see in every stranger
you

# Threshold Blessing

Brigit
Bless this threshold
and all who cross it
those without
those within
those poised above
when all possibility
exists

Bless young dog and old cat
desperate wasp and busy ant
Bless the tiny mites that burrow in their nest

Bless my family and their friends
those who hold our lives
unknown   unthanked
Bless all graces which enter here
and all which issue forth

Bless us in our times of woe
our times of darkened hearts
Bless us in our times of joy
and bless us when we give

## Family Ties

dear Brigits
may the strength of your bond
bind me
sister to sister
tribe to tribe

foster in me the wisdom
the forgiveness
the creativity
to dwell in family
in community
in peace

# Kindling

this kindling sparks in two directions

I strike the match that lights your flame
but look

your flame in return
igniting me

## Relighting the Flame
### (Lá Fhéile Bhríde 1993)

here in my own small room
I light a first
beeswax candle
in your name
(smell this! honey-fresh
fills the soul with flowers
bees)

a dozen friends in their own
small rooms
linked by letters
linked by love
await their turn

that same day   that same year
half a globe away
Catholic sisters light
your flame anew

friends
supporters
– stand of oaks
bubbling wells
Hill of Allen
Curragh plain –
all those paths you walked
wake beneath their feet

unaware
we light the same
good flame

lovers of Brigit
gathering your gleam
into our palms
cast it back into the world

## Above Nature

it is the nature of the dog
to forage any scraps
of the fox   to flee
of the mythic
savage boar
to gore

in Brigit's realm
dog protects corn
fox gambols
for king and crowd
boar grazes snuffling
like any placid pig

such is the power
of the saint

against my nature
to hide   to flee
to sneak   to snatch   to gore
I hear her voice

and like the wild fox
race across the plain
leap into the jumping chariot
shelter
beneath her cloak

prepare to do anything
she wants of me
because I love to do
as she has asked

## Who Tends Her Flame

this one is old (so she tells us)
seldom ventures from her house
sees ice form on boughs
above the passing stream
marks the flight of owls
prays urgently for soldiers
for children
for the soul of a country
(she says) that damns itself

comes to her shift early
leaves late

this one dances in red
grinding lights
song flung across
a throbbing stage
guides her pen over
gaping pages
creamy coffee cold
in her forgotten cup
raises her eyes
to age-dimpled windows

tattoos the knots of Brigit
on her back

this one
toils in church offices
wrestles her child
through pain
addiction

dreams of mossy shrines
and rain-silk hills
she carries her mother
through stroke and cancer
trades stinging words
retreats into her yogic lair
to pray

jests when life tastes bitter
on her tongue

who tends her flame

women   children   men
who await the unexpected
who wish for more for self
for soul   for world
who linger a moment
longer than they must
who when rays of sunlight
strike slanting through shadow

see a bright eye watching
and fiery dancing feet

## Visitor at the Door

I tremble as paper
stirred by a gentle draught

the door of my hut
is open before you

no cloak hangs over it

to muffle the force
of entry

obscure the intensity
of your light

## Whisper/Birth

quietly
(flame burning//night slowly smudging light)
only this small flame
I curl to it

every twenty days your light returns
I its timid usher
(forget//anticipate//feel nothing// fall into
your flame with fresh relief)

mother
you are here again in splendid
silent form
in smallness
(at the hearth of an insect//the bonfire of a flea)
I curl around you
your dog
resting by the only warmth
inside this room

I am going to your birthplace
(the land draws me//draw me in//
draw me out)

I do not know if I will ever be born
(linger in this tear-like womb
suspended over me//not quite touching //
never quite slipped
inside myself)

## Why I Tend Your Flame

why return always
to this endless ritual
of nineteen days plus one

(on the twentieth day of the cycle
when each sister has had her turn
you keep your flame alive

(in the evening of the following day
you offer me the glowing coal
to kindle
my own small fire)

I am so forgetful
I strike the match
and before the wick is blackened
I am a thousand miles away
planning   worrying   angry   wishful
hurrying to accomplish this and that

if I am so very forgetful
why return

in that moment
when I take a breath
place the candle in its lantern
lantern in its cauldron
pour water clean and fresh
around its base
when I add the blue juniper
whisper words of honouring
of sharing   and of blessing

of request
when I open my hands to receive
your eye-bright coal
my heart opens with them
I glimpse this wider land
this wider life
come closer
for one fraction of a second
awake

this is your gift to me

mine to you
is to return
again and again
to this moment of ignition
in my soul

# Shift Day

on this day of guardianship
I wrote to the Daughters
tended the kitten
said goodbye to the old queen
held my mother
played with my nephews
teased my lover
taught a child about candle magic
considered my sister carefully

lift me to the heaven of your brow
O Brigit
on your strong and gentle hand
from there let me bear witness
to goodness in my own soul
and this enduring world
that is our home

## She Receives the Flame

receives the flame from her sister
opens palms
assumes it

planes and curves
of her face
alight

Brigit
Blessed One
Grace-Giving Goddess

receives the flame from her sister
enters heart
thoughts   eyes

all in her regard
blessed
Brigit's flame within

Brigit
Blessed One
Grace-Giving Goddess

receives the flame from her sister
same altar
continents apart

same flame
animating
joyous life

Brigit
Blessed One
Grace-Giving Goddess

Brigit and Her Sisters sit close
share beer and laughter
crucible of creation   sight
healing poem sung on world's wounds

Brigit
Blessed One
Grace-Giving Goddess

Their children
once blessed
give

flame that enters   flame passed on
to next and next and next

Brigit
Blessed One
Grace-Giving Goddess

receives the flame from her sister
from their Goddess receive Her flame
tend it   love it
pass it on

## Suffering and Compassion (Chant)*

the leper
the madman
the starving dog
me    all me

the threshold
the milk
the woman at birth
me    all me

the listening   feeding
the limitless churn
me    all me

I am Brigit
Brigit is me

the leper
the madman
the starving dog
you    all you

the threshold
the milk
the woman at birth
you    all you

the listening   feeding
the limitless churn
you    all you

You are Brigit

Brigit is you

the leper
the madman
the starving dog
the world     all the world

the threshold
the milk
the woman at birth
the world     all the world

the listening    feeding
the limitless churn
the world     all the world

The world is Brigit
Brigit is the world

## Invited to the Feast*

damn

that cauldron of yours
could hold a bull
two maybe

all around its bronze
perimeter beings
thin-armed   huge heads
busy at strange doings
spring out in relief

flames snarl hungry
at its base

when you invited me
to your feast I was enchanted
now I see your iron look
your hook-like hands
you reach and grab me
by one leg and force
me in the pot

this rebirth
is clearly
going to hurt

# Caim of Bride*

standing here I pivot
arm extended
finger straight
your circle to describe

encompass me Bride
all horror exclude
all safety include
harm from within
harm from without
banished
in the clear moving girdle
of your faith

## Brigit Bids Farewell to Her Bishop

kind Conlaeth
dear hermit
well-regarded for your miracles

you were drawn by me
from your wild shelter
to do priestly service to my nuns

greatest smith over all of Ireland
friend of my soul

in stillness your form lies
emptied of nobility
we lay your body by the altar
of the oak

no priest supplants you at my right hand

I am old
old enough to peer through heaven's door
I must look there now
to hear the wisdom of your thoughts
must look into my heart
to find your tenderness

# My Life as a Bird

when at end of life
my spirit is freed and takes wing
I will fly to you
a small wren   a dunnock perhaps
dun brown and barely seen in life
dun brown and barely seen in death
joyful   fruitful
feeding in the shelter of your great tree
polishing my bill against its bark

your work
shall be my enlightenment

I will rest upon your palm
gaze in simple trust
into your labyrinthine eyes

# Endnotes

"A Blessing on Your Nets" – In some areas periwinkles or limpets were left alive in the corners of the house as a blessing on Saint Brigit's Eve (Ó Duinn, *Rites of Brigid*, pp. 23-24).

"All-Giving Sun, Father of Brig" – An early tract calls poetry "a noble woman" who is "multiformed multifaceted multimagical" (Ó hÓgáin, *The Sacred Isle*, pg. 112).

"Appeasement" – In cases where Bride's sign is not discovered in the ashes, Carmichael records the ritual of sacrificing a fowl in this way in order to find favour with her again. This tells us something about how Bride was seen and how her people strove to control the wild elements of their vulnerable lives by bargaining with the saints or deities who held sway. Carmichael says that in different regions either pullets or cockerels were the appropriate sacrifice. I imagined here a speckled fowl, based on the threshold nature of speckles (not white, not black, but both) and the common association in Irish lore of speckled things with the Otherworld – perhaps for that very reason (Carmichael *Carmina Gadelica I*, pg. 169).

"At Battle's Pause" – *Cath Maige Tuired Cunga*, sections 37 and 48, Fraser (1915).

"A Woman With God" – Fleetwood, *History of Medicine in Ireland*, pp. 13-14.

"Bealtaine Cattle Blessing" – Inspired by Robert Gibbings' account of the Bealtaine cattle blessings in Crobdearg, near Rathmore, Kerry in 1949.

"Bean Sídhe" – The shrieking and weeping here refer to Brigit's response to the death of her son Ruadán in *Cath Maige Tuired*:

"125. But after the spear had been given to him, Ruadan turned and wounded Goibniu. He pulled out the spear and hurled it at Ruadan so that it went through him; and he died in his father's presence in the Fomorian assembly. Brig came and keened for her son. At first she shrieked, in the end she wept. Then for the first time weeping and shrieking were heard in Ireland. (Now she is the Brig who invented a whistle for signalling at night.)" *Cath Maige Tuired*, The Second Battle of Mag Tuired translated by **Elizabeth A. Gray**

Isolde Carmody and Chris Thompson, the Story Archaeologists, suggest Brigit as the possible source of the story of the "banshee," literally bean sídhe, woman of the sídhe. See "Revisiting Mythical Women 05: The Search for Brigid" *Story Archaeology* (12 April 2016).

"Booleying Time" – Booleying is summer hill pasturage which allows the valleys to recover their growth of grasses. It takes place from Bealtaine to Samhain (30 April to 31 October); cattle from several herds of connected landholders may be booleyed in common by younger people, usually in single gender groups.

"Brigit Meets the King" – Details of a king's house from Ó Cróinín, *Early Medieval Ireland 400-1200* (pp. 71-74).

"Brigit in the Time Before" – "barrows henges raths" and "souterrain" refer to types of archaeological remains found in Ireland.

"Brigit's Candle Bearer" – The European Goldfinch is called Coinnleoir Muire in Irish. Coinnleoir = Acolyte or Candle Bearer and Muire = Mary. Muire here refers to Saint Brigit, the "Mary of the Gael." Thus, the name of the bird is "Bearer of Brigit's Candle." The candle is her eternal flame, reflected in the goldfinch's red face. There is another, related name for the goldfinch: lasair, f. (gs. -srach, pl. -sracha), meaning "flame, blaze."

"Brigit's Garden" – This poem corresponds to Gort (Garden), a letter in the medieval Irish script called the ogam. The first three lines are translations of the medieval word ogams that apply to it: "milsiu féraib," "glaisem gelta," and "med n-ercc" (Laurie, *Ogam: Weaving Word Wisdom*, pg. 107).

"Brigit's Oaks" – During the Depression the municipality of Saint James, Manitoba, Canada gave permission to its citizens to cut any tree for firewood but the oak, thus ensuring the survival of its venerable urban woodland (Lorraine Arnott, *pers. comm.* (2008)).

"Brigit's Pastures" – Another name for the **Curragh**. (See Glossary). Cambrensis, *Topographia Hibernica* "Chapter XXXVI: Of the hedge round the fire, which no male can enter":

...In this neighbourhood there are some very beautiful meadows called St. Brigit's pastures, in which no plough is ever suffered to turn a furrow. Respecting these meadows, it is held as a miracle that although all the cattle in the province should graze the herbage from morning till night, the next day the grass would be as luxuriant as ever. It may be said, indeed, of them...

'Cropt in a summer's day by herds, the dew's
Refreshing moisture verdure still renews.'

"By Brigit's Day" – Ó Catháin, *The Festival of Brigit*.

"Caim of Bride" – The "caim" is a type of protective blessing common in the west of Scotland. "In making the caim the suppliant stretches out the right hand with the forefinger extended, and turns round sunwise as if on a pivot, describing a circle with the tip of the forefinger whilst invoking the required protection. The circle encloses the suppliant and accompanies him as he walks onward, safeguarded from all evil, without and within. Protestant or Catholic, educated or illiterate, may make the caim in fear, danger, or distress...." (Carmichael, *Ossian Collection* > *Carmina Gadelica, [102], Òrachan* Dìona, Caim, [248]).

"Cattle in Winter" – ricil: f. Rickle, small stack. ~ mhóna: small turf-stack (Ó Dónaill). Tidey: in calf (McGlinchey, *The Last of the Name*, pg. 85).

"Curragh Sacrifice" – This burial mentioned in Ó hÓgáin, *The Sacred Isle*, pg. 47, citing Raftery, Barry. *Pagan Celtic Ireland* (1994) pg. 199.

"Danu and the Dagda" – Ó hÓgáin, *Sacred Isle*.

"Daughter of the Dagda" – Macalister, *Lebor Gabála Érenn*, Vol. 4, pg. 92, 102, 104, 133, 159, 197, 308) and Daimler, *Pagan Portals Brigit*, pg. 27. Re: transgression: violation – MacAlister had "plunder" (pg. 46).

"Divine Cow" – Once again, I am using poetic license. In the *Vitae* the druid feeds her on the milk of a white, red-eared cow. He does not call her from the Otherworld. On the other hand, white animals with red ears are commonly shown to be Otherworldly creatures in Irish myth.

"Dubthach maccu Lugair" – When Saint Brigit's father, Dubthach, son of Demre, wanted to marry her to a suitor, the person selected was another Dubthach, Dubthach maccu Lugair, who was, in hagiography, the representative of the poets (*Oxford online*, Brigit entry, 23 July 2014: http://www.oxforddnb. com/view/10.1093/ref:odnb/9780198614128.001.0001/odnb-9780198614128-e-3427).

"Dubthach Versus the Druid" – Ó hÓgáin, *Sacred Isle*.

"Fionn and Brigit" – Fionn mac Cumhaill had his headquarters at Almu (the Hill of Allen in Co. Kildare. Also called Almha), Ó hÓgáin, *Sacred Isle*, pg. 180.

"Four Corners to My Bed" ("On Lying Down," "On Waking") – Inspired by prayers collected by Hyde, *Religious Songs of Connacht*.

"Grove of a Goddess" – Green, *Celtic Myths*, pg. 66.

"Healing Ways" – Fleetwood, *History of Medicine in Ireland*, pp. 7-9.

"Hostel" – I have taken liberties here, making exceptions in the norms to harmonise the Otherworld and saintly hostels.

"Hungry" – The sacrifice of a fowl was sometimes practised if a family believed they had not received Saint Bride's blessing on Óiche Fhéile Bhríde (Carmichael *Carmina Gadelica I*, pg. 169). See note above for "Appeasement."

"– I'm Asleep and Don't Waken Me –" – With a lift of the cap to the 18th century poet Dennis O Donnell.

"Indictment and Defense" – The whole topic of the Christianisation of Ireland is a messy one, with people often assuming a great conflict and overthrow. A Victorian belief no longer favoured in Celtic and Irish studies supposes a pre-patriarchal egalitarian society, followed by growing oppression of women in Christian times. It seems that in fact Irish women gained greater autonomy under Christianity. See *Women in a Celtic Church: Ireland 450–1150* by Christina Harrington for an excellent discussion both of the shift to Christianity and of our changing modern perceptions of that shift.

"Invited to the Feast" – The images here are inspired by those on the Gundestrup Cauldron, which likely represent deities, including one who appears to be dipping warriors into a cauldron for rebirth. There is no reason to believe the deity in question is Brigit.

"Keeper of Cattle" – "save us from straying/save us from harm": adapted from "Beannachadh Buachailleachd [101]/Herding Blessing." (Carmichael, *Carmina Gadelica* Vol. I pg. 275).

The tradition of offering drops to fairies and then tracing the sign of the cross is attested to by Logan, *The Old Gods: The Facts about Irish Fairies*, pg. 123. According to Logan the belief in fairies began around 700 C.E. (pg. 5) – too late for Saint Brigit to have believed in them, whereas, even if this particular custom does not reach back that far, she would likely have believed in, and perhaps made offerings to, the sídhe.

"Macc Da Thó's Pig" – Gantz, *Early Irish Myths and Sagas*, pg. 187.

"Milk, A List" – The cure for poison is from Fleetwood, *History of Medicine in Ireland*, pg. 4.

"Numinous Land" – Romano-Celtic: The eagle and oak linked to a sun god. Ériu: possibly a sun goddess in the role of sovereignty;

this is part of ritual associated with sacred kingship. A related myth has the sun as a gold cup full of red liquor borne by Ériu and handed to successive mortal kings. Green, Miranda Jane. *Celtic Myths*, pg. 43. Numinous: possessed by spirits;

"Ogam Reading" – Laurie, *Ogam: Weaving Word Wisdom*.

"On the Burren" – Lady Gregory, *A Book of Saints and Wonders*, pg. 8.

"One and Three" – In this poem I am looking at the continental material, specifically sculptures of the *Deas Matronae*, not at literary material of Irish origin. This is not strictly kosher, as there is no reason to assume that all Celts envisioned their gods in the same ways.

"Ordination of Brigit, Bishop" – This poem refers to the story found in Cogitosus of Brigit taking her vows as a nun. Bishop Mel inadvertently consecrates her as a bishop instead, giving her and her abbess descendants greater powers and privileges than those of any other Irish nun. Nevertheless, she doesn't appear to have performed all of the roles of a priest, and once her monastery was established, she sought the aid of the hermit bishop Conlaeth in serving her community.

"People of the Goddess Danu" – The title is one translation of the name of the deities of Ireland, the Tuatha Dé Danann. (See Glossary, "Danu.")

This is only one interpretation of the story. According to Rolleston, d'Arbois de Jubainville speculated that Danu and Brigit may be one and the same, mother of all the gods (Rolleston, pg. 126). In either case, it is through the remnant of Brigit, if indeed she and the saint are closely connected, that our most direct and obvious living connection with the old deities remains.

"Pillars of the World" – MacCulloch, *Celtic and Scandinavian Religion*, pp. 86-87.

"Ridge of Clay" – Withes are generally willow or osier. "Lífé was the old name of the plain of Kildare; and the river flowing through it, anciently called Ruirtech, thus obtained the name of 'Amhain Líffé', or 'River of the Liffé'." "On the Curragh of Kildare," W. M. Hennessey, *Proceedings of the Royal Irish Academy* (1836-1869), Vol. 9 (1864-1866), pp. 343-355.

"Song of Brigit" – Inspired by "Song of Amairgen," as quoted in Rees and Rees, *Celtic Heritage*, pg. 265.

"Suffering and Compassion" – https://soundcloud.com/user-617834076/suffering-and-compassion for melody.

"The Blood-Thirsting Band" – I'm told the correct phrase is "warping" the loom but that would confuse and sounds ill.

"The Curragh of Kildare" – "Broccan's Hymn" and "On the Curragh of Kildare," Hennessy, *Proceedings of the Royal Irish Academy*.

"The Falcon" – From the story of Brigit's falcon as told by the twelfth century writer, Giraldus Cambrensis.

"The Nun Who Races" – *Liber Hymnorum* "The Martyrology of Donegal" states: "The reference to the Curragh is contained in the line 'In Caillech reidhed Currech', i.e. 'the nun who races over the Currech (or Curragh).'

"'The Truth'" – There is little about Brigit as goddess in the medieval texts, and the hints there prove inconsistent – no surprise, when one considers they were written down over centuries, and reflect different times. This poem seeks not to throw over the search for understanding of the texts and their times, but to allow the reader to accept them all as what they are.

"The Well" – The uses of the well referred to here are gleaned from a variety of Scottish locations (MacGregor, *The Peat-Fire Flame*, pp. 144-156).

"Three Brigs and Sencha" – These titles, and this apparent trinity of Brigits, are found in the Ulster Cycle and do not have strict parallels with the triple goddess named by Cormac: patron of poetry, healing, and smithcraft. They may be another example of a triple goddess, especially as the title "Brig of the Judgements" in various stories is applied to all three. In this poem it also suggests a story where the god is married to a triple sovereign goddess who is also his mother and his child. (See **Brig (Other Brigs)** in Glossary).

Ownership: see Ó Cróinín, *Early Medieval Ireland 400-1200*, pg. 131, for details.

"Three Hags" – Ó Duinn, *Rites of Brigid: Goddess and Saint*, pg. 22.

"Three Sisters at Drung Hill" – MacNeill, *The Festival at Lughnasa*, pp. 413, 672, etc.

"Violation" – refers to comments made in the twelfth century by Giraldus Cambrensis regarding the perpetual flame at Kildare (Cambrensis, *Topographia Hibernica* "Chapter XXXVI: Of the hedge round the fire, which no male can enter").

"Walk of the Brigidines" – refers to the annual pilgrimage at

Kildare, organised by the Brigidine nuns at **Solas Bhríde**. (See Glossary).

"Your Feast is Upon Us" – The corn mentioned here is not the maze of the Americas. It refers to the grain of crops such as wheat and barley.

# Reflections in Brigit's Well

# Daily Devotional

One of the elements of prayer I have most felt the lack of is a liturgy for daily devotion. Much as I value free expression and spontaneous prayer, I do best if I also have a framework that fosters internal silence. So I have created one of my own, borrowing ideas from practices developed by the monastics of the Plum Village Vietnamese Zen Buddhist tradition.[1] It is short, as experience tells me that the more complicated I make the procedure, the less I feel like I have time to do it, and the less I practice altogether. I have also discovered that, for me, it's helpful to aim to do it at the same time every day.[2] Once the habit of doing something at a particular time is created it is much easier for me to just go and do it than when I wait for the "right" moment, which, like as not, may never come (though I am flexible on this point). As well, frequent repetition of the same prayers and chants allows me to memorise them, integrate the teachings they express, and move more smoothly into meditative awareness.

On days when I have more time and energy, this short practice can expand to include other chants, meditation, readings, divination, and so on; on days when I have little time, sounding the bell, lighting the candle, and reciting or singing my daily prayer offers a sense of grounding and connection with myself and Brigit, and takes at most five minutes. I suggest going through the stages of the devotional, whichever length you decide on, in an unhurried, contemplative manner, but not to let so long elapse between steps that you lose sense of the movement of the ritual. Of course, if one-part calls to you and you want to stop there and immerse yourself in it, don't feel compelled to carry on. It may be that on this day you do one step only, and that is enough.

About bells: Bells were used in the early Irish church and are another way of signalling that you are entering or acknowledging a sacred space. I use a handmade brass bowl from India – one of the humbler versions – since medieval Irish bells are not easy to come by. Try practicing with your bell until you can find a good, clear tone, striking neither too loudly or too softly. In time your bell will become a good friend to you in moments of worry and distraction, as both the act of inviting it to sound and the sound itself will immediately remind you of the calm that you have created with them in the past.

## *Daily Brigit Devotional*

*Arriving:*

Enter your prayer and contemplation area.

Bow to Brigit. She may be symbolised by an oak branch, a triskele, a rush cross, a drawing, a brídeog. It doesn't need to be expensive or impressive. Something that evokes an essential part of her for you is the best symbol you can use.

Bow to the cushion where you will sit and the altar if you have one. Sit down.

Take three quiet breaths to prepare yourself to invite the bell to sound.

Invite your bell to sound three times, listening to each ring until it ebbs away.

*Lighting the candle:*

Bow again to Brigit and take your matches into your hand, preparing to light the candle. Before striking the match, say:

Brigit
as you bring life to frozen lands

I light your flame
bear your shielding warmth
into this day

(Light the candle.)

*Praising Brigit:*

renewing as the healer's pool
brilliant as the sun among stars
with you  Brigit  I make my home

*Finding a steady posture:*

I sit beneath your ancient oak
upright and at ease
a tall and supple sapling in your shade

*Following the breath:*

the linnet sings
her breath a circle
melodious and fresh

my own breath continues
in softly
out calmly
in
and out
I sit with the silence of my breath

*Fostering mindfulness:*

sensations  emotions

move through my awareness
I watch them tenderly

thoughts gather like clouds
cluttering the sky
returning to my breath
clouds part

*Recitation and/or Song:*[3]

I will kindle my fire this morning
in the presence of Brigit and her holy women.
Brigit, kindle in my heart within
a flame of love to my neighbour
to my foe, to my friend, to my kindred all
to the brave, to the knave, to the thrall
without malice, without jealousy, without envy, without fear
without terror of anyone under the sun.[4]

*Prayer and/or Meditation:*

I structure this part of the devotion differently at different
times. I may sing or recite additional prayers, talk with Brigit,
or, most frequently, sit or walk in silence. If you would like to
learn meditation but don't know where to start, I recommend
the book *Peace is Every Step* by Thich Nhat Hanh. Another
excellent one is *The Miracle of Mindfulness*, by the same
author. A book which offers a beautiful approach to prayer
is *A Book of Hours* by Thomas Merton, edited by Kathleen
Deignan. Merton's writings are selected from and arranged
in private liturgies for intervals throughout the day, for seven
days running.

*Ending the Devotional:*[5]

Invite the bell to sound a final time.
Bow to Brigit and extinguish the candle.

# Endnotes

1. See Nhat Hanh, Thich and the Monks and Nuns of Plum Village (2000). The expression I use in the devotion – "inviting the bell to sound" – comes from Thich Nhat Hanh, who wished for a nonviolent alternative to the idea of "striking" a bell. So, the act is an invitation, and the wooden piece used is the "inviter."

2. I have Clann Dord Fiann of Ireland to thank for this realisation, discovered during the carefully timed twenty-day devotional they organised leading up to Imbolc 2019.

3. I generally sing "I Will Kindle My Fire" (melody available here: https://soundcloud.com/user-617834076/i-will-kindle-my-fire) but I am currently focussing on "Gabhaim Molta Bríde" either alone or with "I Will Kindle My Fire." I recite the English words and then sing the Irish. One version can be found, with pronunciation guide, at http://www.gaolnaofa.org/library/music/gabhaim-molta-bride/, though I prefer to sing the melody offered by Amy Panetta, of the Celtic Feminine Podcast, here: https://www.youtube.com/watch?v=pAoCsHydmQs

4. Original prayer from Carmichael (1900) pg. 231.

5. Optional: I frequently add to the end the devotion by singing "For the River," a song of thanks. It can be found at https://soundcloud.com/user-617834076/for-the-river

# Who is Brigit of Ireland?

Brigit is a multi-faceted figure – or figures. There are different schools of thought about this. Some believe the saint never existed, some that she was initially a pagan and a follower of the goddess Brigit, many more that she absorbed (either in her lifetime or later, in her cult) aspects and traditions of the goddess and came to be a melding of two traditions. Still others see the two as having been entirely separate until confused together by academics in the Victorian era. Personally, I now lean toward the last camp. Yet I don't mourn their cults having become inextricably entwined; they are, for me, in this way enriched.

## Saint Brigit

The Brigit about which the most is known is the saint, born around 450 C.E. or slightly earlier, at a time when Christianity was only beginning to be established in Ireland. Returning Irish converts and continental travellers of the Christian faith had been arriving since the fourth century at least, but only in her lifetime were permanent structures like churches and monasteries built, and she was one of the premiere instigators of that transformation. She died around 530 C.E.

Her best-known foundation was a double monastery at Kildare. It became renowned as a place of learning, where the now-lost illuminated manuscript, the Book of Kildare, is said to have been created. She is described variously as patron saint of dairy workers, Irish nuns, cattle, midwives, newborn babies, and, along with Saint Patrick and Saint Columcille, of Ireland. As we've seen, she was known for her generosity, her unwavering prayerfulness, her clever (and miraculous) ways of solving problems, and her mercy.

Unlike Saint Patrick, Saint Brigit left no writings. Few Irish in her day were able to read or write, barring those trained as monastics, and it is possible she herself never learned. Prayers which are attributed to her, such as that describing her wish to provide a lake of beer to Jesus and other holy beings, were written long after her lifetime.

The first of the *Vitae* (Lives) purporting to tell the stories of her life were written down more than a hundred years after her death, and with subsequent authors they subtly (or remarkably) changed. In modern usage the stories of the different *Vitae* are gathered together, giving her a complex and sometimes contradictory nature.[1] To add to the confusion, her two earliest *Vitae* are named *Vita Sanctae Brigitae* (Life of Saint Brigit) and *Vita Prima Sanctae Brigitae*. *Vita Prima* – the First Life – is now thought to be of later writing than *Vita Sanctae Brigitae*.

In her earliest *Vita*, written by Cogitosus, Brigit is said to be the daughter of "Christian and noble parents," but later *Vitae* depict her mother as her father's slave, and this is the story that is popular today. In the latter version, she became a nun against her father's and brothers' will, having to resort to violence to force their consent. She went on to establish religious communities throughout Ireland, with both women and men in her fold. At some point after her death, her main monastery in Kildare became engaged in a prolonged competition against Saint Patrick's centre in Armagh to become the head of all Irish churches. The story that Cogitosus tells in which, when taking her vows, she was inadvertently consecrated a bishop demonstrates the unusual power that she wielded, particularly for a woman. For centuries,[2] the abbesses that followed her retained greater power than other women religious in Ireland.

In addition to ecclesiastical writings about St. Brigit, tales and practices linked to her are found in all corners of Ireland, while most Irish saints were revered in more localised areas. In a country where only five percent of the saints known to have feast days are women,[3] she is exceptional: widely known, greatly loved and depended upon, her feast day is celebrated on one of the four major seasonal festivals.

Saint Brigit's cult in ancient times grew wherever Irish

monastics travelled, but took especially strong root in Ireland, Scotland, and Wales. In the late twelfth century, in the midst of the Norman Invasion of Ireland, a cleric accompanying the future King John, Gerald of Wales, wrote of a perpetual fire in Kildare which was tended by her nuns. This was finally extinguished during the Dissolution of the Monasteries in the mid-sixteenth century, to be reignited centuries later on Imbolc 1993 by the Catholic Sisters of Solas Bhríde in Kildare and the Neo-Pagan Daughters of the Flame in Canada.

## The Goddess(es) Brigit

Rising in prominence over the past decades is Brigit the goddess, described in *Sanas Cormaic* as three sister goddesses. These sisters, each named Brigit, are the daughters of The Dagda, the Good God[4] of the Tuatha Dé Danann. Their mother is not recorded.

Much less is known about the goddess Brigit than the saint. She is first mentioned in the ninth century. Unlike deities such as her earthy and formidable father, or the awe-inspiring goddess, The Morrigan, Brigit is almost undetectable in the ancient literature. There are, however, three important references: those found in *Sanas Cormaic (Cormac's Glossary)*, in which there are separate entries for the goddess and the saint, in the tale *Cath Maige Tuired (The Second Battle of Moytura)*, and, perhaps, in the *Lebor Gabala Erenn (Book of the Taking of Ireland)*. Together they help us construct some idea of her.

*The Three Brigits, Daughters of the Dagda:*

"Brigid, that is to say, a poetess, daughter of the Dagda. It is that Brigid who is the goddess of poetry and the wisdom contained therein, that is, the goddess whom the poets used to follow. Her craft was magnificent & splendid. Therefore, they called her the goddess of poets, whose sisters were Brigid, the goddess of medicine, & Brigid, goddess of metalwork, daughter of the Dagda; the goddess Brigid was called by these names by almost all of the Irish." *Sanas Cormaic (Cormac's Glossary)* translated by **Antone Minard**

Here we see that Brigit is connected to important and high-status crafts and called on by their practitioners. There were other gods in the old tales who were assigned the title of Smith, Physician, or Poet of the Tuatha Dé Danann, but clearly, she shared those roles in some way, or at some place and time.

The poets of ancient Ireland formed a social class on a level with the king. They bore the knowledge of the people and had the power to raise or lower the fortunes of those on whom they set their poetic sights. Smiths were high status, half-magical persons who remained significant members of their communities until recent times. Healers were an equally important group of individuals, with high honour prices and many laws governing their conduct and responsibilities. Some writers take Cormac at his word and accept the sisters as three distinct beings, but in most works, they are treated as three aspects of the same goddess.

*Brigit of the Cries:*

In *Cath Maige Tuired*, Brig's husband, Bres, is made king of her people. Half Tuatha Dé Danann and half Fomorian, he is beautiful, excellent, and considered a good replacement for the now-blemished king, Nuada. Yet Bres proves so stingy and cruel that the land suffers and a poet satirises him, with war as the inevitable result.[5] Brig and Bres's son, Ruadán, turns against his mother's people, attempting to murder the smith god Goibniu, and is himself killed as a result. In response to this tragedy Brig voices the first keen heard in Ireland, the singing, mournful cry that became a ritual part of Irish funerals for centuries to come. From this fragment of the larger story we can take the image of

241

a mother who, though unable to prevent the conflict that her son is lost in, responds with a powerful voice that resonates throughout time.

Vocalisations such as shouts, whistles, and so on had magical associations in Irish mythology, for instance in the Lia Fáil, or Stone of Destiny, which cried out when a king stood or sat upon it. Brigit herself is associated with vocalisation in a number of ways.

> "Brigit the poetess, daughter of the Dagda, with her were Fe and Men, the two kings of oxen, from whom is Femen [called]. And with her was Triath, king of her boars, from whom is Treithirne [called]. And with her were heard, the three demonic sounds after transgression in Ireland, whistling and weeping and lamentation.

> "And also with her was Cirb king of the rams, from whom is Mag Cirb [called]. With them were Cerman and Cermat and the Mac Oc." *Lebor Gabala Erenn (The Book of Invasions)* translated by **Morgan Daimler**

As Daimler points out,

> "The exact same words are used in Old Irish to describe Brigid's noises when she mourns her son and the noises the animals make when 'transgressions' occur in Ireland – *gol* 'lamentation' or as a verb *golaid* 'weeping', 'wailing' and *eigem* – 'screaming' 'crying in alarm' and also the sound she's said to invent as a warning signal at night – *fet* – is the same whistling sound the animals make as well. So when Ireland is violated with transgressions the three animals keen for the land as Brigid keened for her son. I believe that this can be seen as reflecting the idea of Brigid as a sovereignty Goddess who embodies the land itself, so that transgressions against

the land are violations of the Goddess herself which cause her tutelary animals to keen for her in the exact same manner she mourned her child." *Pagan Portals – Brigid* (pg. 86) **Morgan Daimler**

The fact that Brigit is associated with these sovereigns of their own races, after whom important landmarks are named, supports Daimler's interpretation.[6]

On the other hand, what if it was not the beasts who were making these sounds? I had always assumed from this quote that there were actual demons in Brigit's company in addition to the kings of these beasts. But it could as easily, as sensibly, be read that the sounds come from Brigit herself.

I contacted the Story Archaeologists (Isolde ÓBrolcháin Carmody and Chris Thompson) to ask their opinion:

"... the *Lebor Gabala Erenn* ... shows evidence of post-Norman influenced, synchronistic thinking. So much in the mythology was becoming obscure and unsettling. It was becoming reduced to the status of 'magic' and thus, under church law, demonic.

"This, we have found, was particularly true of the roles of poets and heralds. If their words were 'true' then they could be regarded as prophecy, and if not specifically endorsed by the church, then demonic. It is clearly how the role, appearance, and reputation of Morrigan was altered.

"... [Brig] does play a revealing 'cameo' role in [*Cath Maige Tuired*], which is a much earlier and less synchronistic text. Here, as the creator of 'keening', she has taken on a central poetic role. I am sure you know well, the high status of keening and elegiac poetry in Ireland. It was also closely associated with women. I suppose that offers two reasons why she gets paired with demonic sounds in the *Lebor Gabala Erenn* text ... the ancient significance of keening, poetry beyond words, has become demonic bellowing. Only the connection between keening and sorrow (transgression) has been remembered." *pers. comm.*, **Chris Thompson**

*Brigs of the Judgements:*

Kim McCone points out that "The names Brig and Brigit were prone to interchangeability in early Irish sources…" Some are referred to as goddesses, but others are unproven candidates – women named Brig who may or may not be divine. Lisa Bitel reminds us that the story of Saint Brigit became complicated as her popularity spread. More children were named Brigit, more Brigits entered holy orders and had churches named after them, and so on. So, we must be careful not to assume that every time the name "Brig" or "Brigit" appears we are seeing an instance either of our saint or of our goddesses. Of those who *are* goddesses, it is unclear how many individual deities there are, and how, if at all, they are related to the trio named in Cormac's Glossary.

The most important of these "other" Brigs are the three connected to the famed judge, Sencha (Senchan) mac Ailella, cited in the Brehon Laws (*c.* 700 C.E.).

"The earliest evidence for the goddess is in the Irish vernacular law tracts … which contain a few little legal stories in which Bríg is the daughter, wife, or mother of the legendary judge Sencha of the distant Irish past. According to these she sat by Sencha's side as he made pronouncements on law, and on occasion intervened to correct or contradict him. Nowhere in this material is she equated with the saint of the almost-identical name." *Women in a Celtic Church: Ireland 450-1150* (2002), **Christina Harrington**, pg. 63-63

Eugene O'Curry expands a little on these Brigs:

"Several women of the name of Brig are mentioned in the

ancient laws as female judges; some of them appear to have been connected with each other. The mother of Senchan, chief judge and poet of Ulster in the time of Conchobar Mac Nessa, was called Brig ban Brughad or Brig the female Brugad;[7] his wife was called Brig Brethach or Brig of the judgments; and his daughter, the Brig Ambui alluded to in the text, was also it would appear called Brig "of the Judgments," and was wife of Celtchoir Mac Uthichair, a renowned personage of the Tain Bo Chuailgne, and other heroic tales of that period. She is mentioned as one of the nine, or rather ten, women who accompanied Queen Mugan, wife of Conchobor Mac Nessa, at the Fled Bricrind or Bricriu's Feast." *On the Manners and Customs of the Ancient Irish* **Eugene O'Curry** (1873)

The three Brigs related to Sencha are sometimes confused with each other in the old tales. They are found in the Ulster Cycle and do not have obvious parallels with the three goddesses named by Cormac, patrons of poetry, healing, and smithcraft. They may be another example of a triple goddess, especially as the title "Brig of the Judgements" in various stories is applied to all three, they may be versions of Brigit, patron of poets, suggested by the connection between poets and judges, or they may not be goddesses.

Brig Ambue (Brig of the Cowless) appears to represent a section of society peopled mainly by "the fían or association of propertiless (literally cowless) and predominantly young, unmarried warrior-hunters on the fringes of settled society."[8] Yet she is listed as a jurist. Brig Brethach (Brig of the Judgments), unlike Saint Brigit, who frequently defends oppressed women and slaves, is famous for her wise judgement regarding the rights of freeborn women of property. Brig Briugu (Brig the Hospitaller) was mother of "the Ulster Cycle's peacemaker, Sencha mac Ailella."[9] Hospitality was a vital part of early Irish life, for the fruitfulness of the land depended on the appropriate

245

open-handedness of its king. Hostels were common, and hostellers were expected to welcome all and provide food, shelter, and entertainment. Failure to do so could result in a loss of status.

The Brehon Laws and the part played by Sencha and the Brigs would have been known to the monks who scribed *Cormac's Glossary* in the 9th century. Yet they are not mentioned in the entry on the goddess Brig. This suggests to me that the "Brigs of the Judgements" were not considered by them to be the same as the daughters of the Dagda.

## *Goddess and Saint*

Many of the saint's attributes and traditions have been assigned to the goddess in recent years, based on the assumption that she pre-dated the saint and that her cult was taken over by Saint Brigit or her followers.[10] Lisa Bitel offers an alternative scenario:

"Brigit had not always been a goddess, although there may well once have been a deity or several called Brig. Cogitosus made perfectly feasible arguments for Brigit's authority without invoking literary conventions beyond the traditional Christian canon. However, as Irish religious communities became increasingly hierarchical and competitive, and as women faced growing limits on their authority over sacral spaces and clerical confederations, the writers of Brigit's cult developed new tactics for describing her authority. Hagiographers of the eighth and ninth centuries used traditional motifs of feminine territoriality to reconstruct Brigit. By 900, the nexus of symbols produced the goddess Brigit known in early medieval literature." *Landscape with Two Saints* **Lisa Bitel** (pg. 192)

Regardless of how and when they first intersected, the saint and goddess are intimately connected today, and their devotees vary widely in how they perceive them. Some see one being who embraces the entirety of both, some see two or more distinct entities, and most see a certain amount of blending of the two, whether intentionally or not. The Brigit of today, whether conceived of as saint or goddess, bears strong elements of both.

## Endnotes

1. For a detailed examination of the changes and the reasons behind them see Bitel (2009).
2. This ended in 1132 when, as part of Dermot MacMurrough's bid for power in the region, the abbess of Kildare was raped in order to render her unfit to continue in that office.
3. Statistic from Marcil-Johnston, Liliane Catherine, "The Transformative Nature of Gender: The Coding of St. Brigit of Kildare through Hagiography" (2012).
4. Meaning that he was skilled in many ways – good at everything.
5. In all other tales where Bres appears, he is a valued, even a distinctive member of the Tuatha Dé Danann. For this and other reasons John Carey believes that this tale was a revision written to reflect the pressures of the day, in particular the Viking invasions of Ireland.
6. See Daimler (2016a) for an illuminating exploration of Brigit's appearance in the old texts, and the sources of many of our ideas about her today. For further arguments to support the idea of Brigit as sovereign goddess, see Wolf (2015).
7. Hospitaller.
8. McCone (1990) pg. 163.
9. McCone (1990) pg. 162.
10. This theory has lost ground in modern scholarship. For a detailed examination of the evidence see Harrington (2002).

## Knots in the Weaving: Misunderstandings Along the Way

Morgan Daimler points out a number of confusions that have crept into the story of Brigit in modern times. Some of these have been integrated into personal practice or certain traditions, and have value for many practitioners. The problem is not with that, but with their provenance: they are modern ideas but are often presented as ancient, and when offered as such they confuse an already complicated situation. I will outline them briefly, but encourage you to read Daimler's more detailed account.[1]

### Ella Young, Celtic Wonder Tales (1910)

Ella Young was a poet who, inspired by her Theosophical training, while creatively reimagining Irish mythology envisioned a creation story (something lacking in Irish myth) in which Brigit inspires the gods to make the earth inhabitable. This story, "Earth-Shapers," has become very popular, but it does depart dramatically from both folklore and myth.

### Peter Berresford Ellis, Celtic Myths and Legends (1999)

Ellis also imagined a creation myth for the Irish. In "The Ever Living Ones," older myth is again combined with modern imagination, and Brigit is portrayed as sister and consort of the Dagda, who in the old tales is actually her father. Her role of raising the first keen in Ireland (*Cath Maige Tuiread*) is shifted to the Fomorians.

### Brigit's Mother

Neo-Pagans sometimes assert a mother for Brigit, mostly choosing Boann or the Morrigan, for various reasons. In the texts, only her father, the Dagda, is named, and as his sexual partners were many there is no one goddess over another who can be assumed to be Brigit's mother.

## Maiden, Mother, Crone

Because of the triple nature of the goddess Brigit and the importance of the Maiden, Mother, and Crone in some forms of modern Paganism, many interpret Brigit's triplicity as an expression of that motif. In the Irish texts, though, the three Brigits were sisters, patrons of three skilled and high-status professions, with no apparent difference in age.

Brigit is sometimes placed within this motif as Maiden or Mother, with other goddesses representing the second and third aspects. The Scottish figure known as the Cailleach, or Hag, appears in one apparently recent tale as an antagonist to Bride, where the Cailleach appears to represent winter and Bride the spring. This can be seen as Maiden and Crone.

But, importantly, the motif of Maiden, Mother, and Crone is not represented in Irish or Celtic myth. So, although this can be a powerful idea to work with, it is a modern, non-Irish interpretation. (See *Bride and the Cailleach Are One*, below).

## A shifting in emphasis

Daimler points out that certain aspects of Brigit tend to be retained and valued by modern devotees – her motherly, inspirational, and healing aspects – with a movement away from her martial or agricultural connections.

## Bride and the Cailleach Are One

A "knot" not included in Daimler's list is the idea that these two are youthful and aged versions of one being, a concept gaining acceptance today. Annie Loughlin, in her excellent article, "Bride and the Cailleach," examines the relationship between Bride (Saint Brigit in Scotland) and the Cailleach, a figure of both Scottish and Irish tradition who is generally seen as an old woman. Loughlin explains that this two-aspects, one-being idea is not the usual understanding of their relationship, that, "most traditions in Scotland have them firmly pitted against each other as two differing personalities," where Bride is attempting to bring the warming time of spring to the land and the Cailleach, representing winter, counters with angry blasts of icy air.

She cites Marian McNeill as confirming that, "at least one tradition views Brìde and the Cailleach as being one and the same, with the Cailleach drinking from the Well of Youth at the beginning of each spring, whereby she is transformed into the youthful Brìde." Loughlin goes on to outline the tale, "The Coming of Angus and Bride," from the writing of Donald Alexander Mackenzie: the only source for the details of the tradition. The full text of the book containing this tale is available online, and I have supplied a link in the bibliography.

I would sound a note of caution, though. Mackenzie gives no source for his story, which is written as a well-embroidered fable rather than as clearly evidenced folklore. A prolific Victorian writer and theorist, his ideas frequently had little evidence to support them and some have led to great confusion in later thinking. How much of this tale comes from his imagination and how much from actual tradition we will never know. It appears at any rate to be a relatively modern tradition. (Mackenzie's book was published in 1917).

## The saint is a reworking of the goddess
Another idea not covered by Daimler; I would cite this as a modern convention.[2]

Many people, Christians and Neo-Pagans alike, accept that the triple goddess Brigit is the direct ancestor of Saint Brigit, at least cult-wise – that the saint, if she existed at all, has taken on the traditions of the goddess Brigit. It is speculated that: the holy wells dedicated to Saint Brigit, which are especially abundant in Ireland, were once dedicated to the goddess she replaced; the goddess comes from a time when Celtic women were more equal in status and power to men, freer than they became in Christian times; the goddess Brigit has her origins in a time before even this somewhat more egalitarian patriarchy of Celtic Ireland, one when the goddess, and women, were valued above all.

It has been suggested that the saint herself was initially a druid in the goddess Brigit's cult, taking on her goddess's name, perhaps as a title, and that she and her fellow female druids tended the perpetual flame in Brigit's name. When forced to convert, directly or by pressure of circumstance, and become Christian nuns, the order then continued the practice until the suppression of the monasteries.

This idea, that Saint Brigit was a descendant or a follower of the goddess, is a modern one, arising from the suppositions of Victorian authors whose ideas on the matter, never supported by hard evidence, were based on a variety of assumptions about the inevitable development of society and religion from a more primitive, female-centered stage to a more evolved, male-centered stage.

Christina Harrington, in *Women in a Celtic Church: Ireland 450-1150* (2002) explains the situation well. In her introduction to the book she offers a detailed "academic historiography" in which she examines the path of European scholarship that led to the image of Celtic Christianity and medieval Ireland from which our popular beliefs sprang. In it, she demonstrates how changes in the dissemination of scholarly ideas to the public left us heavily dependent on assumptions no longer accepted by academics. The Victorians expressed their ideas about the evolution of religion and culture, the place of women in early society, the romanticism of the Celts, and so on in the form of books that were easily accessible to the public. Later scholars have tended to publish in obscure academic journals in increasingly specialist language. And so, the interested reader continued to turn to older works, which by now are often no longer in copyright and are available free online or as inexpensive books.

Devoting several pages to Saint Brigit and Kildare, Harrington addresses and dismisses, finding no evidence to support them, the ideas that the saint and the goddess are closely linked, that the saint may once have been a druid priestess tending a perpetual flame, and that the flame itself dates from Saint Brigit's day or reflects either a pre-Christian or a primarily feminine activity.[3] The one point of connection she sees between the goddess and the saint is in their patronage of women.

Increasingly, Neo-Pagan scholars themselves are pointing out inconsistencies in the popularly accepted story of Brigit. In their lively and detailed podcast "Revisiting Mythical Women 05: The Search for Brigid," for instance, the Story Archaeologists, Chris Thompson and Isolde ÓBrolcháin Carmody, compare what evidence they can find of the goddess with the cult of the saint, and find little overlap. Carmody concludes, "... you can't necessarily extrapolate a pre-Christian goddess Brig from the traditions associated with Saint Brigit even if those traditions have pre-Christian roots ..."

That there was in early medieval Ireland a belief in a goddess – or three – by the name of Brigit seems likely. That there was a Christian woman named Brigit who became known as a saint seems so as well. The notion that the cult of one or all of these goddesses was transfigured into that of Saint Brigit, in light of modern scholarship and my own reading of the texts, to me does not.

Whatever our evidence for or our theories about an ancient lineage for a goddess named Brig or Brigit, it is clear that for fifteen hundred years or thereabouts Brigit has been seen as a saint and a woman, and not a goddess. It is true that the authors of *Cormac's Glossary* (*Sanas Cormaic*) wrote of a triple goddess Brigit in the 9th century, but she is not linked in that text to Saint Brigit, about whom there is a separate entry. The medieval and early modern Irish, if they were even aware of Cormac's goddess, turned to the saint for matters practical – a blessing on a fishing boat – and divinatory – a hint of how their fortune would run in the coming year. In practice, because we assume the saint is modelled on the goddess, we are inclined to attribute to the goddess associations that belong to the saint, and which look "pagan" to our eyes. So that in the end our goddess is to a large extent modelled on the saint, rather than the other way around.

Even writers who see a close connection between the two don't automatically ascribe every tradition accorded to Saint Brigit to the goddess (as I in my innocence have done in a number of these poems). The festival of Imbolc, for instance, is often said to be the feast of the goddess Brigit, but there is nothing linking the goddess to any particular feast day, whereas Saint Brigit has many traditions connecting her to Imbolc.[4] As Harrington points out:

"The saint's feast day fell in Imbolc, the official start of spring in the native Irish calendar. *Cormac's Glossary* has an entry on *imbolc*, defining it as 'the time the sheep's milk comes', but does not identify the festival with Brigit. Care of sheep was a specifically women's activity in early Ireland, and there are stories of Saint Brigit shepherding and making dairy products, but it must be remembered that the girl, as the daughter of a slavewoman, is portrayed doing what non-noble girls would do normally. Nowhere, in fact, is Imbolc said to be the festival of the goddess Brigit, and beyond that, the goddess's attributes do not include sheep care. It is only the connection to women that is marked." *Women in a Celtic Church- Ireland 450-1150* **Christina Harrington** (pg. 65)

The word Imbolc, which is debated still but which may mean, according to different authors, "in the belly" or "lactation," appears to refer to the main association Saint Brigit has with the day: the beginning of spring, the time when plants, wild and domestic animals, and humans begin preparations for the burgeoning and sustaining of life.

The goddesses are connected to cultural arts, and perhaps to sovereignty; the saint to fertility and springtime. But in modern Neo-Pagan and even in much Christian practice the attributes of the two are generally blurred together, and a single unified Brigit emerges who lays claim to them all. This is perhaps simply an extension of the process that has been ongoing in culture for all of human existence: the adaptation of old views and traditions into new forms through the blending of cultures and the alteration of ideas. There is nothing wrong with this process of change. But it is useful to be aware of our roots, and thus to be able to make informed choices as to how we see Brigit, and how and whether we extend ourselves toward her.

In the end, although I *see* the saint and goddess(es) in their myriad different roles, in my heart I do address Brigit as Goddess, and although I accept that there are at least two, and perhaps four or even more distinct Brigits, they overlap greatly within my discernment of her. My understanding, though imperfect and, in another's eyes, perhaps quite wrong, is enriched immeasurably by having stopped to truly acquaint myself with the details of each Brigit, and each aspect of any of them which I can find to contemplate.

## Endnotes

1. Daimler (2016a) pp. 53-56.
2. See "The Perpetual Flame at Kildare" below for one vivid example of this convention.
3. See "The Perpetual Flame at Kildare," below.
4. Its other name makes this very clear: Oiche Féile Bríde (the Eve of Saint Brigit's) or La Féile Bríde (Saint Brigit's Day).

## The Perpetual Flame at Kildare

And what of Brigit's flame, this central aspect of her modern cult? In medieval times it was tended by her nuns; now it is kept by lay Christians and Neo-Pagans, as well. As mentioned above, many of us believe that Saint Brigit tended the perpetual flame with her sisters, and that it was a holdover of pagan practice – that she may have been a druid dedicated to the goddess Brigit, possibly one who converted to Christianity.

The evidence against this scenario is substantial, whereas to date, none has been found to support it.[1] Classical writers speaking of the Celts nowhere mention the tending of perpetual flames. The earliest "Life" of Saint Brigit, written by Cogitosus, a monk in her tradition, was composed not much later than 650 C.E.,[2] around a century after her death. It describes Kildare and St. Brigit's church in detail, yet no mention is made of fire-tending. Nor is there reference to a Brigidine perpetual flame in any *Vitae* ("Lives"), hymns, prayers, annals, or texts of any kind until the late 12th c., approaching seven centuries after Brigit died.

We learn of the practice of tending a perpetual flame in Kildare from the Romanised Welsh Briton, Giraldus Cambrensis (Gerald of Wales). In the wake of the Norman invasion of Ireland, as a royal clerk, he accompanied the son of King Henry II, the future King John, on a military expedition to Ireland from 1185 to 1186. The journey resulted in two books, *Topographia Hibernica (Topography of Ireland)* and *Expugnatio Hibernica (Conquest of Ireland)*. He wrote of Kildare:

"The nuns there, nineteen in number, take turns tending a perpetual flame in a sacred place surrounded by a hedge, a place which no man may enter without risking madness or worse. On the twentieth day, though no one touches it, the fire burns on and no ash builds up, for it is tended by the long dead founder of the order, Saint Brigit herself." *Topographia Hibernica* **Giraldus Cambrensis**

Various writers have pointed out that Cambrensis or his informant seems to have relied on stories of the Vestal Virgins for some of his details of Brigit's nuns in this description. Seán Ó Duinn wrote, "It is difficult to know if Giraldus Cambrensis was influenced by the Classics when describing St. Brigid's perpetual fire, but it is strange that he mentions the number 20 as the number of nuns – the same number from which the Vestal Virgins of ancient Rome were chosen. In Ireland, one would expect the number 9 to predominate."[3]

Seven other perpetual flames are known from 12th and 13th century Ireland; all of these were tended by monks, rather than nuns.[4] Ritual and household fires were lit from them: if a household's fire was accidentally extinguished, it would be relit from the fire at the church. Of the hearthstone at Inishmurray, W.G. Wood-Martin wrote that "… fire was always kept burning by the monks for the use of the islanders. In later times, when monks no longer inhabited the cashel, whenever a householder wanted kindling for the family fire, a sod of turf or a piece of wood deposited on this holy hearth ignited spontaneously."[5]

As it is in many religions, fire is important in Christian iconography. It represents both the Holy Spirit and light. Jesus describes his followers as the light of the world and God is a "consuming fire." It's not surprising then, that Saint Brigit's fire associations have equivalents in the Lives of male Irish saints.

"Lord who enterest my members
  Like the embers Thou dost shine,
Take my soul from out my bosom,
  Cleanse from stain and make it Thine." *from* "Thanksgiving After Communion"[6] *The Religious Songs of Connacht*,
**Douglas Hyde, ed.**

Taken together, the evidence strongly implies that the perpetual fire tended at Kildare was of very late date, part of a more common

Christian practice that emerged long after the death of Saint Brigit, not a practice that she, let alone previous worshippers of the goddess Brigit, would have taken part in.

Nevertheless, Kildare's perpetual fire was tended for centuries. It was first extinguished in 1220 by order of Henry de Londres, archbishop of Dublin, only three decades after Gerald of Wales wrote about it. It was later renewed and continued to be tended until ca. 1540 when, during King Henry VIII's Dissolution of the Monasteries, it was once again snuffed out.

In time, the Sisterhood of Saint Brigit died away, to be revived at the invitation of Daniel Delany, Bishop of Kildare, in 1807. Brigidines nuns soon spread from Ireland to Wales, England, the United States, Mexico, New Zealand, Australia, Kenya, and Papua New Guinea. In 1992 Sisters Mary Minehan and Phil O'Shea were, in Sister Mary's words, "asked to come to Kildare and to explore our Celtic Heritage – to reclaim Brigid of Kildare in a new way for a new millennium."[7] They called their home there Solas Bhríde (Brigit's Light). On Imbolc 1993 Brigit's flame was rekindled in Kildare by Sister Mary Teresa Cullen, then leader of the Brigidine sisters, at the opening of a conference, "Brigid: Prophetess, Earthwoman, Peacemaker," organised by *Action from Ireland*, a justice, peace, and human rights group.

Since that day, Neo-Pagans, Christians, and Christo-Pagans of many stripes have tended Brigit's flame, and no longer only women, but men and non-binary folk, too. So, however and whenever Brigit's flame came into being, and whatever the original boundaries that surrounded it, it has broken through those bounds to burn in countless and varied hearts.

## Endnotes

1.  If one day an archaeological dig were conducted in Kildare, at the site of the fire temple, perhaps some of our uncertainties could be answered at last.
2.  Connolly and Picard (1987) pg. 5.

3. Ó Duinn (2005) pg. 64.
4. Harrington (2002) pg. 66.
5. Wood-Martin (1902). See Laurie, Erynn Rowan (2015) for a fuller discussion of the matter.
6. Hyde (1906) pg. 401.
7. Interview with Mary Minehan. http://www.tallgirlshorts. net/marymary/sistermary.html

# A Way Forward

I devoted decades of prayer, service, and study to a Brigit whom I considered a unity of goddess and saint. I believed that the perpetual flame tended at Kildare was a practice that reached back to Saint Brigit's time and possibly beyond; its extinguishment during the suppression of Catholic monasteries was what prompted me to initiate Daughters of the Flame. Having revisited the poems I've written about Brigit, I find that though they still speak to me, often powerfully, in a number of cases I no longer see her exactly as I did when I wrote them. While they reflect diverse ways she has been seen and aspects she has been associated with over time, I have come to accept that some of the fundamental ideas that once seemed clear to me are wrong – or at best have little or no evidence to support them – ideas I painstakingly gleaned, worked with, and integrated into my spiritual life.

Saint Brigit, it seems, was simply a Christian woman who worked hard to assist other Christians, to build religious communities for them at a time when they were very few. The miracles and so on which accrued to her after her death appear in the main to be the natural result of the process of hagiography, which elevates the saint as a means of teaching Christian principles, and of ecclesiastical competitiveness, rather than direct echoes of her pagan past. Where does this leave me?

The Brigit I have found through all my searching, as these poems express, reveals endless riches in every strand of her tapestry. Without rejecting the significance of each version of Brigit in the lives and hearts of her devotees, without rejecting how each version has impacted my own life and guided my spiritual path, for the integrity of my devotion I have had to address this loss and, where necessary, relinquish cherished beliefs in favour of a subtler truth. The poems, however, stay as they began. To alter them would misrepresent my journey with her.

My devotion remains pretty much as it has been: characterised by study, service, and affection, with the flame as a poignant and steadying practice. Although I now differentiate between the two streams of Brigidine cult, they run side by side in my heart. I still think of Brigit as "she" more than "they," while accepting that "they" is the more accurate term. More precisely than before, I address Brigit the goddess or Brigit the saint, Brigit the poet or Brigit the hospitaller, yet I still tend *her* flame. I am no longer fazed by the contradictions, knowing that she has unfolded over many centuries and been envisioned by thousands of people in a myriad ways throughout our changing times. I no longer need to push my understanding of Brigit into a rigid, pre-shaped form. This is a victory for me. It has been a long road to being able to embrace both uncertainty and paradox, to not need things nailed down in a certain way, to be right or wrong, true or false, clearly comprehensible. I still struggle with it in some ways, but I am grateful to Brigit for this gift.

But if Brigit the goddess is not the origin of the perpetual flame, if its tending is not rooted in an ancient pagan practice, does this render Neo-Pagan flame-tending invalid?

I believe it does not. We may as individuals wish to examine anew our commitment to the flame and ask ourselves if it's a practice we wish to continue, if it still holds meaning for us, even if it is of Christian and not pagan origin, even if it is "only" a thousand or so years old. For me, it absolutely does. Tending her flame, whether in the name of the saint or the goddess or both, is a valid and powerful offering that strengthens us as individuals and as a community. And we need not fear finding inspiration in one who is thoroughly Christian, as well as in another who is pagan indeed.

Religions alter over time; religious practices do as well. Our perception of and relationship to the divine changes as our perception of our world changes. Like any other faith, Neo-Pagan religions contain errors and truths; as we find the courage to look deeply into our religions and into ourselves, they and we grow and endure.

If some of our ideas about her are based on out-dated theories, then we discover that we are not so much reclaiming a blessed antiquity as creating a new vision. This is not a defeat, but a liberation. The better I understand what's come before, the broader my present becomes. The more we understand, the better we may craft a spirituality that is rooted in our ancestors but responds to new ideas of, for instance, equality and nonviolence. This is the basis of Reconstructionist religion: understanding the ancestral community as well as possible and then bringing the fruits of that community into the present in ways that make sense for modern times.

It is difficult, sometimes disappointing or even painful, to alter our views on things so personal and precious, but I don't think it needs to lead to a loss of intimacy or profundity or joy, or a lessening of the depth of our spiritual experience. If a Christian comes to believe that Jesus's birth was not actually miraculous, does she need to divorce herself from her religion? If a Buddhist comes to think that the Mara which the Buddha fought beneath the bodhi tree was not a separate, supernatural being but the misunderstanding and grasping of his own mind, does he walk away from his spiritual path?

No. Understanding our religion can only support it. And if Brigit the saint was never influenced by a cult of Brigit the goddess, in her lifetime or for centuries afterward, she has been now. If there was no goddess-centred flame-tending practice in early Ireland, there is now. The saint and goddess will always be connected in the minds of modern devotees to one degree or another, and we will each choose where we sit with these new understandings of her.

Brigit is not going away. Whatever the chronology of her past, her present is vibrant and life-giving. We can do our best to know and learn from her history, but, in the end, it is how we approach her now, and how we embody her in our lives, that matters most.

Neo-Pagans and Celtic Christians will continue to grapple with the issues surrounding Brigit in whatever ways we are willing to do so. Increasingly, we will engage in solid scholarship, unearth genuine traditions, and build our own, modern response to them. And there will always be disagreement.

Brigit the goddesses did exist – do exist. But they are not the saint, and a careful untangling of their aspects and stories from hers can lead us down an exciting and flexible path. We do not need to rely on the particular guardianship, fertility, and generosity of the saint to appeal to the passionate grief or intense patronage of the goddess, nor vice versa. We can honour them all for what they truly bring to our lives without mixing them together. Or we can embrace the blended traditions, whether because we reject the scholarship or simply because we feel most comfortable devoted to a Brigit who combines both the goddesses and the saint.

There is such undepletable richness in Brigidine devotion. I will continue, joyfully, to embrace both the elements of the goddess and those of the saint, from the tender to the harsh, all of which bolster my relationship to the divine, to my spiritual community, to the world, and, without question, to myself. Like a family member whose past is not exactly how I imagined it, Brigit remains my beloved. I regret nothing of my time with her and am thirsty for more. I await further inspirations, further understandings, further gifts. I embrace the ripening of our relationship into peaceful co-existence. And I look forward to the ever-changing presence of Brigit in our world.

Blessings of Brigit on you and yours, on all you craft and all you heal. May the spirit of generosity and the energy of springtime fill you. May you find your voice, your fire, your deepest well, and may Brigit, however you know her, walk with you all the days of your life.

Beannachataí Bhríde ort.
Brigit's Blessings on you.

Mael Brigde
Imbolc 2020
Vancouver, B.C.
Canada

# Afterword by Morgan Daimler

Mael Brigde's *Sun Among Stars* is an essential weaving together of poetic inspiration, personal experience, and Brigid herself. Having read this book, you have travelled along a pathway with the author, learning about who this enigmatic and powerful goddess is not from cold facts but from the heart of someone who has a strong connection to the source. It is at once contemplative and deeply personal, educational and reflecting the evolution in understanding and belief that we all go through over time. For this alone it is an invaluable addition to the corpus of material on Brigid.

Brigid is immensely popular but also mysterious. People seek her as a Christian saint and as a pagan goddess and find a tangle of mythology and folklore that sometimes clearly delineates the two figures and sometimes conflates them, leaving the seeker to sort out on their own where the truth may lie. Stories about her can be contradictory and even difficult to understand yet they all hold the same essence, the same heart to them, reflecting Brigid in her many roles. Seeking and questioning, trying to explore Brigid's nature, is the beginning and the end of finding her because eventually we realise that it is through questioning that we create our own ever-changing understanding of her.

This text has, perhaps, framed the truth in the most direct way by capturing Brigid's essence as we have it today in all her contradictions and certainty. Brigid is a pagan goddess, a poet, smith, and healer, mother of sons who die by violence. Saint Brigid is a miraculous figure, liminal in her heritage and early life, stronger in many ways than the famous saint Patrick. These two seemingly very different figures overlap and complement each other, so that ultimately any quest for a pure figure on either side of the religious divide is reducing Brigid to one dimension. Such reduction is a mistake.

Brigid is a complex figure and only by understanding that complexity can we ever hope to understand who and what Brigid really is. Trying to reduce her into one thing or another loses too much of what uniquely makes her herself, and in minimising her we devalue her. Following the liminal route laid out by the stories and poems here leads the reader to seeing Brigid holistically. Because, ultimately, she contains the goddess who the Daughters of the Flame lit their candles for and the saint who the Brigidine nuns kindled a flame for, and it is no coincidence these both occurred on the same date in the same year. She is each, she is both, and she is beyond both in the sense that she is beyond our human capacity to fully understand.

You have read through this work by Mael Brigde and hopefully it has spoken to you on some level. Brigid's voice is an active one, whether it is whispering in your dreams or singing in your imagination. Read this work again and sit with the words of the poems that speak the loudest to you. Let the goddess or the saint or simply Brigid speak to you through the author's words as you step into a deeper understanding of Brigid over and over again and allow that understanding to grow and change with each reading.

This is the beginning of something more, not the end.

# Glossary

**Ale.** Both **Brig Briugu** and **Saint Brigit**, in their roles as **hospitallers**, have connections to ale, a weak brew which was the most important drink of its day, due to the possibility of illness borne in untreated water. Children and adults alike drank it, and in normal amounts it did not lead to drunkenness – indeed it is an important ingredient in healing, as seen in incidents in Brigit's Lives where ale is sought for an injured person, and the refusal of it is seen as a breach of hospitality.

Saint Brigit is well known as ale-woman in Ireland, Scotland, and Wales, and a medieval poem is credited to her (though likely to have been composed in the 8th century – long after her death) which expresses a desire to have a lake of ale at which Jesus and all the saints might drink their fill.

I should like a great lake of ale
For the King of kings.
I should like the family of heaven
To be drinking it through time eternal.[1]

Mac Neill notes that Brigit's well at Liscannor is the site of "one of the three most strongly lasting survivals of Lughnasa,"[2] and is known as "Brigit's Vat" (Daigh Bhríde – a reference perhaps to the ale vat, as opposed to the cauldron used for cooking meat.

**Almu.** (Hill of Allen) *See* Curragh, The.

**Ambue.** *lit.* cowless. One without property. (*See* **Brig (Other Brigs)**).

**Anam Cara**. Soul friend. A creation of the Irish monastics, a soul friend is a spiritual guide from whom nothing is kept secret:

a confessor whose concern is for the wellbeing of one's soul, not simply the enforcement of regulations. Saint Brigit is said to have told a young man whose soul friend had died that he must not eat or rest until he had found another anam cara, for a person without a soul friend is like a body without a head. This Irish concept transformed the act of confession in the Church as a whole from an occasional, public, sacrament to one held in private and focussed on the personal spiritual needs and abilities of the person confessing.

**Animals**. Several animals are particularly linked to Saint Brigit through her Lives or folklore, including the oystercatcher, goldfinch, linnet, swan, fox, wolf, cow, sheep, and bee. Her strong association with the dairy makes cattle her primary animals, and she is said to visit homes on Saint Brigit's Eve (Óiche Fhéile Bhríde) in the company of her cow, who is featured in her iconography. The red-eared cow whose milk was her only sustenance after weaning suggests an Otherworldly connection; in the Irish tales Otherworld animals are frequently described as white with red ears. The goddess Brigit is said to have had four animals – the king of rams, the king of boars, and two kings of oxen (*Lebor Gabala Erenn*).

**Bealtaine**. 31 April-1 May. One of the four **Quarter Days**.

**Boann**. Irish goddess, after whom the River Boyne was named.

**Booleying**. (Irish: búaile: 'cattle enclosure.') Summer pasturage in the hills to allow the valleys to recover their growth of grasses. It takes place from Bealtaine to Samhain; cattle from several herds of connected landholders may be booleyed in common by younger people, usually in single gender groups.

**Brat**. Cloak, mantle. In more general application covering, cover;

cloth, etc. (eDil: dil.ie/6568).

**Brechtnat**. Wife of Saint Brigit's father, Dubthach.

**Bres/Eochaid Bres**. Brig's husband, father of Ruadán; it is not stated to which Brig, daughter of the Dagda, he was married. Half-Fomorian, half Tuatha Dé Danann, he replaced Nuada as king of the Tuatha Dé Danann after the first battle of Mag Tuired. As a Fomorian he brings agricultural knowledge to the craft- and magic-wise Tuatha Dé Danann. In my interpretation he is a **threshold** deity. See *Cath Maige Tuired* and *Cath Maige Tuired Cunga* for two different impressions of Bres. See also Wolf (2015).

**Brian, Iuchar, Iucharba**. Three sons of Tuireann, also called the "Three Gods of Skill." In *Lebor Gabála Érenn* they are said to be the sons of Danu; in *Immacallam in Dá Thuarad*, the sons of Brig and Bres (Carey, pg. 56).

**Brídeog**. A ceremonial image of Saint Brigit, traditionally carried from house to house on **Lá Fhéile Bhríde**, demonstrating her blessings on that night.

**Brig (Other Brigs)**. The three additional Brigs or Brigits most often suggested as goddesses are all related to Sencha the judge. They are sometimes confused with each other in the old tales. They are most commonly referred to as Brig Ambue (Brig of the Cowless), Brig Brethach (Brig of the Judgments), and Brig Briugu (Brig the Hospitaller). These names, and this apparent trinity of Brigits, are found in the Ulster Cycle and do not have strict parallels with the three goddesses named by Cormac, who were patrons of poetry, healing, and smithcraft. They may be another example of a triple goddess, especially as the title "Brig of the Judgements" in various stories is applied to all three. *See* **Fianna**.

**Briugu.** "Landowner, hospitaller, in later sources also farmer, yeoman. In legal texts the briugu is a rich landowner with a public function of dispensing unlimited hospitality to all persons in his hostel, which must be in an accessible position. For this he is given the same honour-price as the king of a túath... (b. recognised as common intervener in disputes)" (eDIL: dil.ie/6874, accessed 30 May 2020). This refers to *free* classes of people; the unfree classes, from serfs to slaves, were not extended this hospitality. *See* **Brig (Other Brigs): Brig Briugu, Hospitality,** and **Hospitaller.**

**Broicseach.** Mother of Saint Brigit.

**Cath Maige Tuired.** Second Battle of Moytura. Bres, husband of Brig, daughter of The Dagda (it isn't specified which of the three sisters is meant), is elected leader of the Tuatha Dé Danann. His misrule leads to crisis and war. Ruadán, son of Brig and Bres, is killed. Brig raises the first keen in Ireland. (Read also *Cath Maige Tuired Cunga* for a different view of Bres. *See* Wolf (2015) for a greater exploration of the story and the characters of Brig and her family. (Clearly, here I have only picked out of a very rich story the bits that pertain to Brig).

**Celts.** The term "Celt" is a wobbly one, and when it comes to the Irish as Celts, it gets even wobblier. Some researchers think it wrong to apply the word widely to Iron Age Europeans, where others are convinced by the archaeological, literary, and linguistic evidence. Certain scholars embrace the term in its application to the Irish, while others reject it, describing native Irish culture as a unique blend of pre- and post- Celtic influences, with the Celtic element strong but not overarching.

That said, the term is generally presumed to apply to the peoples, and their material culture and language, who occupied much of northern Europe between about 600 B.C.E. and 600 C.E. These people had influence throughout Europe, even to the sacking of Rome in the early 4th c. B.C.E. and Delphi a century later. They settled widely, from Ireland in the west to Scotland in the north, and east as far as Asia Minor. They were composed not of one united empire but of numerous and varied tribal groups, such as the Gauls in what is now France and the Picts in what is now Scotland, with trade, conflict, and cultural exchange between tribes and between themselves and their neighbours. The conquest of Gaul by Caesar and Britain under Augustus led to a hybrid culture in these areas, with elements of Celtic tradition mingling with new ideas from Greece and Rome. The Romans did not succeed in conquering Scotland and Ireland, although they certainly would have had history not taken a turn in the 5th c. C.E. and pulled their attention back to the continent. With the collapse of Rome, the Celts also disappeared everywhere but in the far west of Europe. Today six key areas remain that identify as Celtic: Ireland, Scotland, Wales, Cornwall, the Isle of Man, and Brittany (Green, 1996).

**Clootie**. Prayers left in the form of cloths tied around the branches of trees near Saint Brigit's wells. (Note that indiscriminate tying of cloths and other materials to trees has led to extensive damage where thoughtlessly done. One person's offering can become another person's environmental travesty).

**Cogitostus**. Believed to be a monk at Kildare approximately a century after the death of Saint Brigit. Author of her earliest Life, *Vita Sanctae Brigitae*.

**Conlaeth**. Saint Brigit's bishop at Kildare. A hermit before being persuaded to join her, he was famous for his metalwork.

**Coracle/Currach**. Wicker-framed boat, originally covered in skins. These crafts are extremely mobile in the sea and thus are excellent for fishing and require great skill in handling.

**Cormac mac Cuilennáin.** Bishop and chieftain of Leinster, he is the purported author of *Sanas Cormac* (*Cormac's Glossary*). A ninth century document, it is more likely to have been written by multiple monastic scribes. It gives the first account of a goddess named Brigit, in the person of the three goddesses who were daughters of The Dagda.

**Cross.** Brigit's crosses are woven from rushes or straw at **Imbolc** and placed over doorways in houses and byres for protection. Common throughout Ireland, they have many forms, though in modern times, perhaps due to the public radio and television company RTÉ adopting it as their logo some decades ago, the four-armed cross is now the best known and most copied outside of Ireland. E. E. Evans supposes that the three-armed Brigit's cross, generally reserved for the protection of the cattle and the threshing, is of greater antiquity than the four-armed varieties. There is no reason to suggest it was connected to the triple goddess, but I did take that liberty in "Shadow Harvest."

**Curragh (of Kildare), The.** A plain of common land between Kildare and Newbridge, stretching to approximately 2000 hectares. In elder times it was called Cuirreach Life, suggesting it may once have reached the banks of the River Liffey. At one end of the Curragh stands the Hill of Almu (Hill of Allen). Fionn MacCumhail dwelt in Almu before Saint Brigit's birth, and she would have been aware of his stories. The Curragh has long been a military assembly and training area and is famous for its racehorses.

**Currach.** See **Coracle/Currach.**

**Curragh Wrens.** Poor Irish women who attached themselves to the English soldiers stationed on the Curragh in the 1800s. They lived in poverty and ostracism, and the English public was alerted to their plight through the efforts of Charles Dickens and James Greenwood.

**Dagda, The**. The Good God, called this because he was good at everything (see *Cath Maige Tuired*). Father of the three goddesses named Brigit. His club was able to kill with one end and with the other, restore to life.

**Dairy**. Bathed in milk at her birth, employed as a dairy maid, Saint Brigit has many miracle tales involving the dairy. Butter and milk were important in Irish society and she had particularly strong associations with them.

**Danu**. Tuatha Dé Danann is commonly assumed to mean "People of (the Goddess) Danann/Danu" but may mean "People of Skill" or "People of Craft." See *Story Archaeology*, "Stories of Creation." https://storyarchaeology.com/stories-of-creation/

**Darlugdacha**. A nun in Saint Brigit's order and her close friend. According to the Benedictine Monks of St. Augustine's Abbey (Ramsgate, England) in their *Book of Saints* (1921), she was the successor of Saint Brigit as Abbess of Kildare. (Died C.E. 524). Some writers assume a lesbian relationship between them but this is not clearly supported. Possibly they were anam cairde (soul friends), judging by their closeness and Saint Brigit's emphasis on the necessity of a soul friend.

**Dair**. Oak. A revered tree through much of Europe, it is associated with Kildare – Cill Dara or the Cell (or Church) of (the) Oak – Saint Brigit's home monastery. However, it appears the name refers to a church built from oak, not a church associated with a sacred oak grove, as previously assumed. One of the **ogam feda** is named after this tree.

**Dubthach**. Saint Brigit's father. "Brigit (was the) daughter of Dubthach, son of Demre (or Dreimne), son of Bresal, son of Den, son of Conla, son of Artair(?), son of Art Corb, son of Cairpe the Champion, son of Cormac, son of Oengus the Dumb, son of Eochaid Find Fuathnart, son of Fedlimid the Lawgiver, etc." (Source: "On the Life of St. Brigit (*Leabhar Breac*)" (Translated by Whitley Stokes) [Corpus of Electronic Texts Edition])

**Éire/Ériu**. Ireland. (Also, a goddess, and mother of Bres).

**Famine. The Hunger.** The Irish Famine is one of the most profound occurrences in Irish history, with its effects still being felt today. At least a million people starved and another million emigrated, reducing the population from eight to six million between 1845 and 1850. The causes were not entirely simple. Ultimately, though, a failure of the moneyed classes to effectively respond to a virulent potato blight – in many cases capitalising on the plight of impoverished tenants by evicting them – resulted in far greater damage to individuals and communities than would otherwise have happened. Passage overseas was offered as an escape from starvation, with hundreds of thousands sailing on what came to be known as Coffin Ships. Promises of food and water were not fulfilled, and fever swept through the filthy, over-crowded ships. Those who survived often found themselves turned away on reaching port, out of fear of the illness the boats carried.

**Feda**. See **Fid**.

**Fid**. Letter of the Ogam. *Plural*: feda.

**Fianna**. Landless warrior bands living on the outskirts of formal society, loyal to the king and to their leader, the greatest of whom was **Fionn MacCumhaill**. These bands were not outlaws or itinerant poor, but played a key role in ancient Irish society, the sons and sometimes daughters of kings and nobles who generally reintegrated with the tuath when they were old enough to acquire property and take on a mature role in society.

**Fionn MacCumhail.** In Irish heroic legend, Fionn was the leader of the Fianna. The collective tales of Fionn and the Fianna are referred to as the Fenian Cycle. These tales of Leinster in southern Ireland contrast with the northern heroic tales of the Ulster cycle.

**Fir Bolg.** The fourth invasion force to Ireland. They fought the Tuatha Dé Danann at the first battle of Mag Tuired, who drove them off to the Aran Isles. It was in this battle that King Nuada lost his arm and Bres replaced him. (*Lebor Gabála Érenn* [*Book of the Taking of Ireland*])

**Fire.** Fire is an important component of the Celtic religious worldview, as of course it is of most cultures. Fire is strongly associated with Saint Brigit and can also be linked to the three goddesses who share her name, through its obvious uses in smithcraft and healing, and through the "fire in the head" achieved by the greatest poets in ancient times.

Saint Brigit, in folk practice, is intimately concerned with the hearthfire; one of the signs of her having blessed a house on her feast night is the mark of her foot or staff in its ashes. A column of fire ascended from the saint's head at her consecration, just as a column of fire blazed from the hut where she lay undisturbed as a child (*Bethu Brigte*). In a later story she is said to have accompanied Mary into the church for her rite of purification after the birth of Jesus. To distract curious eyes from the shy Mary to herself, Saint Brigit wore a crown of candles on her head. It is for this reason that she is associated with the Marian feast of Candlemas, on 2 February.

Gerald of Wales (*Giraldus Cambrensis*) visited Ireland in the twelfth century with the aim of writing a travelogue that would help to justify the recent invasion of Ireland by the English. His rarely flattering and regularly fanciful depiction of Ireland and its people remains contentious to today. Yet he did speak glowingly of Kildare and the stories of Saint Brigit he encountered there, reporting among other things an illuminated manuscript from the Kildare scriptorium that must have rivalled the Book of Kells. He also described a perpetual fire kept by nineteen nuns in St. Brigit's order. The fire, which no man might look on, was tended on the twentieth day by the long-dead saint, apparently a continuation of a practice from her day, six centuries earlier.

Many writers have been certain that this reflects a much earlier pagan practice, and refer to the remarkably similar practices of the Vestal Virgins of Rome. Others are not convinced, pointing out that Gerald of Wales could easily have modelled his story on those very Vestal Virgins. Fire, such a basic element in all life, is as important a symbol in Christianity as elsewhere, and there were at least seven other monasteries in Ireland in the 12th and 13th c. that tended a perpetual flame – in each case by men. Most importantly, there is no mention of a special fire of any sort by Cogitosus, who described Saint Brigit's monastery in detail five hundred years before Gerald's time, nor is such a fire mentioned in any of her other Lives or lore. The perpetual fire in Kildare must have been a very late addition, part of a Christian practice that arose at that time. Nevertheless, the perpetual flame speaks deeply to Neo-Pagans as well as Christians and flame-tending has become an important part of modern Brigidine practice.

**Fish/Fishing**. Saint Brigit is called upon to bless fishermen's nets and boats. Garments blessed on her night are worn by some fishermen, and preparations for the season are made on her feast day.

Small white fishes occur in relation to Saint Brigit in some folklore, particularly associated with healing – for instance, the rare sighting of one of these fishes in the rocks of the Burren on her day means the pilgrim will be healed.

**Fomhoire/Fomorians**. "Under-demons" or "latent-demons" who occupied Ireland from a time before the first invasion and never left it. Brig's husband Bres was half Fomhoire, half Tuatha Dé Danann, as was Lug. (*Lebor Gabála Érenn* [*Book of the Taking of Ireland*]).

**Gerald of Wales**. (Latin: *Giraldus Cambrensis*) Author of *Topographia Hibernica* (*Topography of Ireland*) and *Expugnatio Hibernica* (*Conquest of Ireland*).

**Glannad**. Smoke used as offering or for purification. Laurie, Erynn Rowan (2007).

**Goibniu**. The smith god of the Tuatha Dé Danann.

**Glas Goibniu**. The smith god's cow, "Goibniu's Grey."

**Gort**. Garden. Another **fid** of the **ogam**.

**Healing**. One of the three arts connected with the triple goddess Brigit, daughter(s) of The Dagda. Saint Brigit is also strongly associated with healing.

**Hospitality, Saint and Goddess**. A key feature in Iron Age social and religious life, generosity in all its forms is a hallmark of Saint Brigit. In her tales she gives food, material objects, time, and advocacy, particularly in defending the marginalised. When she gives things away, particularly those which don't belong to her, her prayerful devotion to God results in the food and some of the objects being replaced. People around her – her father, her sisters in religious life, for example – are often frustrated by her generous habits and try to stop her. As well, her monastery was frequently visited by travelling bishops, etc., who were always welcomed by her.

It may be that hospitality is an important feature of the Goddess Brigit, as well, if we accept that the poorly known figure Brig Briugu is a manifestation of Brigit. Certainly, the Dagda, father of the three sisters Brig who are connected to the cultural arts, is strongly associated with generosity, particularly in the motif of his cauldron, one of the four treasures of the Tuatha Dé Danann. No one ever went away from it unsatisfied.

**Hospitaller.** An important role in ancient Irish society, played by a wealthy landowner whose hostel was always open to travellers, where food and comfort were lavishly provided, as indicated by one hospitaller's cauldron, said to be large enough to accommodate an ox and several pigs. A failure to provide could cause loss of face, whereas continuous demand on supplies could lead to financial ruin. Nevertheless, it was a very high-status occupation and such hostels are frequently the site of Otherworldly interference in the tales. The role of hospitaller began to be assumed by monasteries as they became a feature of the Irish landscape, and stories of housing and entertaining travelling bishops, for instance, are prominent in Saint Brigit's stories. See **Brig (Other Brigs): Brig Briugu**.

**Imbas**. Supernatural enlightenment. Ecstatic inspiration. A high ideal of the poet.

**Imbolc/Imbolg/Oimelc.** One of the four great "Quarter Day" festivals dividing the Irish year seasonally. Imbolc (sundown 31 January until sundown 1 February) marks the beginning of spring. The festival has at least since the 9th c. been connected to Saint Brigit, who is said to have died on that date.

Lá **Fhéile Bhr**íde/Óiche Fhéile Bhríde. Saint Brigit's Day/Saint Brigit's Eve. When the saint returns to this world and goes from house to house dispensing blessings. See **Imbolc**.

**Lebor Gabala Erenn**. (*The Book of the Taking of Ireland*). Dating to the 11th century, the book describes several waves of invasions of Ireland, ending with the Gaels, or Milesians – the "Sons of Mil."

**Lives**. Accounts of the life and miracles of Saint Brigit. The primary Lives include the earliest, by **Cogitostus**, *Vita Sanctae Brigitae*. *Vita Prima Sanctae Brigitae* is so named because it was once thought to be older. The third, *Bethu Brigte*, is also called the Irish Life for having been written in Irish, not Latin.

**Lug/Lugh**. An important Irish god. A latecomer to the Tuatha Dé Danann, he assumed their leadership to defeat the Fomorians in the Second Battle of Moytura.

**Lus**. Flame – Herb. A fid of the ogam.

**Macha**. Irish goddess. She married a mortal man who bragged of her running ability to the king, who then forced her to race against his horses in spite of her being pregnant. At the end of the race she gave birth to twins, and laid a curse on the Ulstermen that they would suffer the same pangs she had whenever they were needed in battle.

**Maige Tuired**. The plains where two major battles were fought between the Tuatha Dé Danann and the Fir Bolg (in the *Cath Maige Tuired Cunga* [*First Battle of Moytura*]) and between the Tuatha Dé Danann and the Fomhoire (in the *Cath Maige Tuired* [*Second Battle of Moytura*]). Maige Tuired (Magh Tuireadh/Moytura/Moytirra) means "plain of pillars" or "plain of towers." It refers to two separate places in Connacht; the first is near Cong, County Mayo and the second is near Lough Arrow in County Sligo.

**Morrigan, The**. Irish goddess knowledgeable in magic and battle.

**Multiplicity**. An important feature of Celtic mythology, not fully understood. It at minimum strengthens by amplifying. One of the most common forms of multiplicity is triplicity. The goddesses Brigit are three sisters, daughters of the god The Dagda. Saint Brigit's original gathering of women religious equalled ten – herself and nine others – in keeping with the sacredness of three and its multiples.

Though in common parlance treated as one goddess, in Cormac's glossary (9ᵗʰ c.), the situation is different. Daughters of the Dagda, the three sisters, each named Brigit, have individual areas of patronage, one of healing, one of smithcraft, and one of poetry. It is perhaps an artifact of our millennia of monotheism that despite referring constantly to her as a triple goddess, we relate to her as a single goddess with three spheres of influence.

**Name (Brigit)**. *Brigit* is the earliest known form of her name in Ireland, Latinised as Brigitta. The pronunciation is hard on both the *g* and the *t*: *Brig* as in "wig" and *it* as in "it." I use this spelling and pronunciation, not because they are "right," or "best," but because I feel comfortable with them.

Fairly early on in the records the final "t" in her name became a "d" and the Latin form, Brigida. In modern Irish the name has softened to *Brighid*, (genitive *Brighde*), pronounced BREE-ud. Other forms include *Bríd* (BREED), as well as *Bride* (BRIDE) and *Bridey* (BRIDE-ee), which are most common in Scotland, and the Welsh *Ffraid* (FRI-uhd).

However, *Bridget* (BRIJ-ut) is the most common form, in Ireland and elsewhere. This variant entered Ireland from Sweden due to the similarity of Saint Brigit's name to that of the Swedish

Saint Bridget. It is not, as has been asserted, connected to the various place names in Ireland containing the word "bridge." This comes instead from the anglicising of Irish names. For instance, *Droichead na Banna* becomes, in English, Banbridge. On the other hand, places with the root "Bride" are connected to Saint Brigit, such as "Kilbride" (Cell or Church of Brigit).

**Osier**. Willow used in basketry and as wattles.

**Ogam**. A simple Irish alphabet consisting of twenty letters (feda, singular fid). The letters in general have names with distinct meanings attached to them, such as "sulphur," "soil," etc. Often used today for divination.

**Ogma**. Inventor of the ogam. Brother of the Dagda and therefore Brigit's uncle.

**Onn**. Foundation – Wheel. A fid in the ogam alphabet.

**Otherworld**. The realm of the deities and possibly the dead. Usually seen as a supernatural place of youth, beauty, health, fruitfulness, and happiness. It can be visited by chance or through the intervention of an Otherworld being. Time moves very differently there, and a visitor may return – if they return – to find centuries or seconds have passed. It is a liminal, or threshold, place, entered through burial mounds or caves, on hilltops, under water, or by travelling the western sea.

**Pagan vs. pagan**. In this manuscript I have capitalised Pagan when it refers to a modern practice or religion, and left it lower case when it refers to the broad swathe of pre-modern practices and religions.

**Palladius**. First bishop of Ireland. He was born in Galatia ca.

363 C.E. and died ca. 450 C.E., perhaps three years before Saint Brigit was born. (By comparison, Saint Patrick was born ca. 383 C.E. and died 17 March 461 C.E., when she was about ten years old).

**Plants**. Saint Brigit's plants include the dandelion, daisy, and other sun-faced flowers, the snowdrop, thought to be the first flower of spring and blossoming on her feast day, the bay laurel, the oak, and the windflower or "Brigit anemone."

**Poetry**. One of the three arts connected with the triple goddess Brigit, daughter(s) of The Dagda. The poets of Ireland were the holders of the people's history and genealogies, and were the most powerful persons apart from kings. The best of them had access to Otherworldly inspiration and were capable of making or destroying others with their words.

**Pratie**. Potato.

**Púca/Pooka**. A fairy horse.

**Quarter Days**. The four Quarter Days in the Irish Calendar. They are Samhain, Imbolc, Bealtaine, and Lugnasad. Each is associated with a change in season and agricultural activities, and three of the four – all but Imbolc – are associated with bonfires as well.

**Realms (Three)**. The Celts, including the Irish, acknowledged three vital realms: land, sea, and sky. Where they did not fear defeat in war, they did fear the rising up of these elements, and would swear by them as by the gods their people swore by.

**Ruadán**. Son of Brig and Bres. In the Second Battle of Moytura he is turned against his Tuatha Dé Danann kin and attempts to slay Goibniú, the Tuatha Dé Danann's smith god, in order to aid the Fomorians. Goibniú kills him in self-defense. See *Cath Maige Tuired* and "The Mythical Pairing of Brig and Bres," Wolf, Casey June (2015).

**Saint Brigit, Cultural Spread**. Though known largely as an Irish Catholic saint, Saint Brigit is also beloved of Protestants – The Cathedral Church of St. Brigid, Kildare, with its famous round tower and fire temple, belongs to the Church of Ireland – as well as Orthodox Christians, who are responsible for many of the beautiful icons of her that we encounter online. Geographically, she is important in Ireland, Scotland, Wales, and to a lesser extent in England, Italy and Portugal, as well as other sites in Europe, where medieval Irish monks brought her veneration and even a portion of her relics. Wherever her diaspora has settled, Saint Brigit has come, as well, such as Ontario and Quebec, in Canada. With the general popularisation of the saint she is becoming more important in churches which have no particular connection to her homelands, a recent example being the *St. Brigids Eucharist*, an LGBTQ-affirming ministry at Christ Church Cathedral in Vancouver, Canada.

**Serpent**. Though nowadays a popular motif connected to Saint Brigit, she is not connected in ecclesiastical literature or folklore to snakes in Ireland, which lacks snakes entirely. (Contrary to the legends of Saint Patrick, there were never any there to drive away. The connection with snakes is found in Scotland, where the appearance of the serpent on her day is seen as a sign of spring. See *Carmina Gadelica*).

**Shawly**. An old term for the Irish peasant women who wore shawls as part of their customary garb.

**Síd/Sídhe/Síth**. (Often spelled in English without the fada [accent] on the i). The Otherworld dwellings of the Tuatha Dé

Danann, most frequently in mounds, beneath the ground. Also sometimes used as a name for the Tuatha Dé Danann themselves, who are known as the People of the Sídhe. Fionn MacCumhail's sid, Almu, is in the Curragh inside the Hill of Allen.

**Smithcraft.** One of the three arts connected with the triple goddess Brigit, daughter(s) of The Dagda. Saint Brigit's bishop, Conlaeth, was also a renowned smith. Smithcraft is important in warfare, for the making of weaponry, but also in hospitality, for cauldrons, ale vats, and so on. The crucible is an important symbol of transformation.

**Solas Bhríde.** "Solas Bhríde is a Christian Spirituality Centre which welcomes people of all faiths and of no faith. The Vision of the Centre is to unfold the legacy of St. Brigid and its relevance for our time." (Source: Solas Bhríde website: http://solasbhride. ie)

It is also the home of the Irish Brigidine Sisters who rekindled Saint Brigit's flame in 1993. It is in Kildare, Éire.

**Sons of Míl/Milesians.** The Gaels, sixth invaders of Ireland. They invaded in response to the murder of Íth, son of a Milesian king Breogán, by three Tuatha kings. They are the third people the Tuatha Dé Danann do war with.

**Sovereignty Goddess.** Common in Irish mythology is the goddess who represents in part the physical land and its dominion. Rule of Irish society rested upon sacred marriage between her and the king, and offense to the land resulted in his unseating.

**Spring.** Saint Brigit is associated both with the beginning of the season of spring (**Imbolc, Lá Fhéile Bhríde**) and with springs and healing wells.

**Sun**. Brigit is not generally believed to be a solar goddess. Saint Brigit, on the other hand, as initiator of spring has solar elements in both her folk tradition and *Lives*, for instance the sunwise weaving of her crosses and plentiful associations with the eye, sun-faced flowers such as dandelions and daisies, etc. The famous story of her hanging her cloak on a sunbeam is found in Cogitosus.

**Torc**. Gold neck ornament worn by wealthy Iron Age Celts.

**Threshold**. Brigit is seen in many ways as a liminal, or threshold, being, and this symbolism is important in modern-day Brigidine devotion. She appears as both goddess and saint, representing a threshold between two largely exclusive forms of religion, and a door through which Neo-Pagans and Christians may reach out to each other. As a saint, she returns bodily from heaven each spring to bless the farms and households of those who welcome her – a practice not widely known among saints, who may be prayed to in heaven and intervene on our behalf, but who don't physically return. This is similar in effect to the appearance of Irish Otherworld beings in the old tales, whose movement into this world makes the Otherworld accessible to humans. A number of other threshold images arise in her Lives, beginning with her mother giving birth to her as she crouched with one foot in and one out of the house.

Threshold moments are important in our lives. They are times and places when we can move in one direction or another, be one thing or another, and even more, where we can see in two ways at once. Brigit's comfort in this realm makes her of great help in our spiritual evolution. (See also **Bres**).

**Tuath**. People, tribe; territorial unit of ancient Ireland.

**Tuatha Dé Danann**. Fifth invasion force to Ireland. Fought Fir

Bolg in first battle of Mag Tuired, Fomhoire at second battle of Mag Tuired, and later the Gaels. In each of the second two battles they won some aspects of the battle and lost others. (*Lebor Gabála Érenn – Book of the Taking of Ireland*)

**Vitae**. See **Lives**.

**Warfare**. Where the goddess Brigit of the smiths is clearly linked to warfare, and the possible goddess Brig Ambue may be connected to the warring bands called the fianna (see **Reflections in Brigit's Well: The Goddess(es) Brigit)**, Saint Brigit has been called upon to bless Leinster in battle. She has also gone out of her way to prevent bloodshed in her tales.

**Water**. Many holy wells in Ireland are dedicated to Saint Brigit. She is most often connected with springs coming up from the earth as opposed to rivers or the sea. (See **Clootie**). The breaking up of the ice on inland waters is sometimes seen as Brigit wakening the **spring**. (See **Realms (Three)**.

**Well of Wisdom**. At the Well of Wisdom of Irish myth, nine hazels grow. When their nuts fall into the water, the salmon eat them. Anyone eating the salmon ingests the wisdom contained in them. When fire and water mingle they form mist, which in Irish mythology represents a gate to the Otherworld. (Laurie, Erynn Rowan. *Ogam: Weaving Word Wisdom*.) These are not connected to Brigit in the literature but I take the poetic liberty of doing so because of Brigit's connections with wisdom, wells, and poetry.

## Endnotes
1. Translation by O'Curry, "Great Lake of Ale" in Curtayne (1955), pg. 78-79.
2. Ibid pg. 275.

# Pronunciation Guide

Irish pronunciation is a challenge for those who have not grown up around the language. The letter sounds do not correspond entirely to English sounds, and non-standard spellings and word forms, plus differences between Old or Middle Irish and Modern Irish, can complicate things further. Rather than attempt a complete pronunciation guide, I will offer rough approximations of some of the most common terms used in the book, and then urge you toward other sources.

| Word | Pronunciation | Meaning |
|---|---|---|
| bandia | BAHN-JEE-uh | goddess |
| Bealtaine | BYAHL-tuh-nuh | 1 May |
| beannachtaí | BYAN-uhkh-tee | blessings |
| bean sí | BAN SHEE | fairy woman |
| bile | BILL-uh | sacred tree |
| Brigit | BRIG-it / BRIDG-it | Brigit |
| Bride | BRIDE | Brigit |
| Bhride | VREE-dyuh | Brigit |
| Brugh na Bóinne | BRU NA BOHNYE | Boyne valley tombs |
| cara | KAH-ruh | friend |
| dia | DYEE-UH / JEE-uh | god |
| draoi | DREE | druid |
| draíocht | DREE-uhkht | druidry, magic |
| file | FILL-uh | poet |
| filíocht | FILL-ee-uhkht | poetry |
| Imbolc | IM-uhlk | Seasonal Festival on 31 January – 1 February |
| Lá Fhéile Bríde | LAW AY-luh BREE-dyuh | Festival of Brigit on 31 January – 1 February |
| Lúnasa / Lughnasadh | LOO-nuh-suh | Seasonal Festival on 31 July – 1 August |
| Oíche Shamhna | EE-huh HOW-nuh | Samhain Eve on 31 October |
| tobar | TOE-buhr | well, spring |
| Samhain | SOW-uhn | Seasonal Festival on 31 October – 1 November |
| sí | SHEE | fairy mound |

# Irish Language

Those who wish to delve more deeply into the Irish language will find many aids online.

*A Beginner's Guide to Irish Gaelic Pronunciation:* http://standingstones.com/gaelpron.html

*Abair.ie:* Trinity College Dublin's recorded pronunciation dictionary. You may download words in mp3 or WAV formats. http://www.abair.tcd.ie

*Bitesize Irish Podcast:* https://www.bitesize.irish/subscribe-to-podcast/

*DuoLingo:* offers a popular free online Irish course. https://www.duolingo.com/course/ga/en/Learn-Irish
Irish president Michael D Higgins praised the work of DuoLingo volunteers and pointed to the success of the project as "an example of what can be achieved quickly." "*Ar fheabhas!* President praises volunteer Duolingo translators," by Éanna Ó Caollaí. *The Irish Times* Fri, Nov 25, 2016.

*eDIL:* The Electronic Dictionary of the Irish Language is a digital dictionary of Old and Middle Irish. It is based on the Royal Irish Academy's *Dictionary of the Irish Language.* http://edil.qub.ac.uk

*Forvo:* "Irish pronunciation dictionary." Many though by no means all Irish words are recorded, sometimes by several speakers. https://forvo.com/languages/ga/

*FutureLearn - Irish 101: An Introduction to Irish Language and Culture* (followed by a number of other sections up to 202 at the moment and perhaps more in future): Dublin City University developed and teaches these excellent courses through FutureLearn. https://www.futurelearn.com/courses/irish-language

*Sabhal Mòr Ostaig:* has a brief and useful page, "The Pronunciation and Spelling of Modern Irish" at http://www.smo.uhi.ac.uk/gaeilge/donncha/focal/features/irishsp.html

# Bibliography and Suggested Reading

An Claidheamh Soluis [Ireland], Jan. 25, 1908. Quoted in "St. Brigid in Tradition and Art," *The Furrow* Vol. 3, No. 2 (Feb., 1952), p. 4. Quoted by Marcella in Trias Thaumaturga. http://triasthaumaturga.blogspot.com/2015/02/saint-brigids-feathered-servant.html

Bitel, Lisa M. *Landscape with Two Saints: How Genovefa of Paris and Brigit of Kildare Built Christianity in Barbarian Europe.* Oxford University Press (2009).

Cahill, Thomas. *How the Irish Saved Civilization.* Anchor [New York] (1996).

Cambrensis, Giraldus. *The Topography of Ireland* translated by Thomas Forester; revised and edited with additional notes by Thomas Wright. In parenthesis Publications [Cambridge, Ontario] (2000). (Original name: *Topographia Hibernica* (1188)).

Carey, John. "Myth and Mythography in 'Cath Maige Tuired,'" *Studia celtica* 24/25 (1989/1990) 53-69. University of Wales Press [Cardiff].

Carmichael, Alexander. *Carmina Gadelica Volumes I* and *II.* T. and A. Constable [Edinburgh] (1900). (The *Carmina Gadelica* is Alexander Carmichael's collection of the prayers and miscellaneous lore of Gaelic-speaking Scotland, gathered between 1860 and 1909). http://www.sacred-texts.com/neu/celt/cg.htm

Curtayne, Alice. *St. Brigid of Ireland.* Browne & Nolan [Dublin] (1955).

Daimler, Morgan. *Pagan Portals – Brigid: Meeting the Celtic Goddess of Poetry, Forge, and Healing Well.* Moon Books [New Alresford, England] (2016a). (Daimler's examination of the texts, ancient and modern, that have shaped our understanding of Brigit are particularly useful).

Daimler, Morgan. *Pagan Portals – Gods and Goddesses of Ireland:*

*A Guide to Irish Deities*. Moon Books [New Alresford, England] (2016b).

Daimler, Morgan. *Pagan Portals – Irish Paganism: Reconstructing Irish Polytheism*. Moon Books [New Alresford, England] (2015).

Danaher, Kevin. *The Year in Ireland: Irish Calendar Customs*. The Mercier Press [Cork / Dublin] (1972). (Annual feasts, celebrations, and practices in Ireland).

Danaher, Kevin. *Irish Country People*. Mercier Press [Cork / Dublin] (1966), pg 16.

Danaher, Kevin. "Irish Folk Tradition and the Celtic Calendar." *The Celtic Consciousness*. McClelland and Stewart [Toronto] (1981).

Duffy, Joseph. *Patrick in His Own Words*. Veritas [Dublin] (2000).

eDIL – Electronic Dictionary of the Irish Language (edil.qub. ac.uk). Queen's University Belfast.

Egan, Ann. *Brigit of Kildare*. Kildare County Council Library and Arts Service [Ireland] (2001) (novel/poetry)

Fleetwood, John F. *The History of Medicine in Ireland*. Browne and Nolan [Dublin] (1951).

Fraser, J. "The First Battle of Moytura." Ériu v.8 (1915), pp. 1-63 [H 2.17]. School of Irish Learning [Dublin]. (This is *Cath Maige Tuired Cunga*).

Gantz, Jeffrey. *Early Irish Myths and Sagas*. Penguin Books [London] (1984).

Gibbings, Robert. *Sweet Cork of Thee*. Dutton [New York] (1952).

Green, Miranda Jane. *Celtic Myths*. University of Texas Press [Austin] (1995).

Green, Miranda J. *Dictionary of Celtic Myth and Legend*. Thames and Hudson [London] (1992).

Green, Miranda J. "Who Were the Celts?" from *The Celtic World*. Routledge [London] (1996).

Gregory, Lady. *A Book of Saints and Wonders*. Dun Emer Press [Dundrum, Ireland] (1906).

Hahn, Thich Nhat. *Peace is Every Step*. Bantam [New York] (1990).

Hahn, Thich Nhat. *The Miracle of Mindfulness*. Beacon Press [Boston] (1975).

Hahn, Thich Nhat and the Monks and Nuns of Plum Village. *Plum Village Chanting and Recitation Book*. Parallax Press [Berkeley] (2000).

Harrington, Christina. *Women in a Celtic Church: Ireland 450–1150*. Oxford University Press (2002).

Hennessy, W. M. *Proceedings of the Royal Irish Academy* (1836-1869), Vol. 9 (1864 - 1866), pp. 343-355. Royal Irish Academy [Dublin].

Hyde, Douglas. *Religious Songs of Connacht*. Irish University Press [Shannon] (1906 [1972]).

Joyce, P.W. *The Wonders of Ireland*. Longman's, Green, and Company [London / New York] (1911).

Kelly, Fergus. *A Guide to Early Irish Law*. Dublin Institute for Advanced Studies (1988).

Kissane, Noel. *Saint Brigid of Kildare: Life, Legend and Cult*. Four Courts Press [Dublin, Portland, U.S.A.] (2017).

Koch, John and Carey, John, ed. *Celtic Heroic Age*. Celtic Studies Publications [Aberystwyth, Wales] (2003).

Kraus, Erin. *Wise-woman of Kildare: Moll Anthony and popular tradition in the east of Ireland*. Four Courts Press [Dublin, Portland, U.S.A.] (2011).

Laurie, Erynn Rowan. *Ogam: Weaving Word Wisdom*. Gardners [Stafford, England] (2007).

Laurie, Erynn Rowan. "Queering the Flame: Brigit, Flamekeeping, and Gender in Celtic Reconstructionist Pagan Communities," *The Well of Five Streams: Essays on Celtic Paganism*. Megalithica Books [Stafford, England] (2015).

Letts, Winifred Mabel. "Saint Brigid" (poem). Cuala Press [Dublin].

Logan, Patrick. *The Old Gods: The Facts about Irish Fairies*. Appletree Press [Belfast] (1981).

Loughlin, Annie. "Brìde and the Cailleach" (2016-2018). *Tairis: A*

*Gaelic Polytheist Website.* 29 May 2020.

Macalister, R.A.S., ed. *Lebor Gabála Érenn: The Book of the Taking of Ireland,* Irish Texts Society [Dublin] (1941).

Mac Cana, Proinsias. *Celtic Mythology.* Chancellor [London] (1970).

Mac Cana, Prionsias. "Aspects of the Theme of King and Goddess in Irish Literature," *Etudes Celtiques* 7 [Paris] (1955) 76-114 and 356-413.

MacCulloch, J.A. *Celtic and Scandinavian Religions.* Hutchinson's Univ. Libr. [London] (1948).

MacGregor, Alasdair Alpin. *The Peat-Fire Flame.* Ettrick Press [Edinburgh] (1947) pp. 144-156.

Mackenzie, Donald A. *Scottish Folk-Lore and Folk-Life.* Blackie [London] (1935) quoted in Tairis "The Year in Scotland."

Mackenzie, Donald Andrew. "The Coming of Angus and Bride," *Wonder Tales from Scottish Myth and Legend* (1917) pp. 33-48. https://www.sacred-texts.com/neu/celt/tsm/ tsm05.htm

Mac Mathúna, Liam. "Irish Perceptions of the Cosmos," *Celtica* 23. Dublin Institute for Advanced Studies (1999).

MacNeill, Máire. *The Festival at Lughnasa.* Oxford University Press [London] (1962).

McCone, Kim. *Pagan Past and Christian Present in Early Irish Literature.* An Sagart [Maynooth, Ireland] (1990). (Particularly "Fire and the Arts.")

McGlinchey, Charles. *The Last of the Name.* J.S. Sanders & Co. [Nashville, U.S.A.] (1999).

Melissa. "Interview with Sr. Mary Minehan," *Slí na mBán: The Road of Women: journeys with Irish women activists* [website] (2/19/99). (Accessed 29 May 2020). http://www.tallgirlshorts. net/marymary/sistermary.html

Merton, Thomas. *A Book of Hours,* ed. Kathleen Deignan. Sorin [Notre Dame, U.S.A.] (2007).

Meyer, Kuno, ed. and trans. "Hail Brigit: An Old-Irish poem on the Hill of Alenn." From *The Book of Leinster*. 1.7148-25. M. Niemeyer (1912).

Minard, Antone, trans. "Brigit Conference Handout" containing *Sanas Cormaic* Brigit reference: "Deconstructing the Dagda: Towards an Understanding of the Gods in Medieval Irish Literature" (2013).

Minehan C.S.B., Rita. *Rekindling the Flame: A Pilgrimage in the Footsteps of Brigid of Kildare*. Solas Bhride Community [Kildare, Ireland] (1999).

Nagy, Joseph Falaky. *The Wisdom of the Outlaw: The Boyhood Deeds of Finn in Gaelic Narrative Tradition*. Four Courts Press [Dublin, Portland, U.S.A.] (1985).

O'Brien, Lora. *A Practical Guide to Irish Spirituality*. Wolfpack Publishers [Strokestown, Ireland] (2012).

*Celtic Way of Life*. O'Brien Press [Dublin] (1998).

Ó Catháin, Séamas. *The Festival of Brigit*. D.B.A. Publications Ltd. [Dublin] (1995).

Ó Cróinín, Daíbhí. *Early Medieval Ireland 400-1200*. Routledge [Abingdon, England] (1995).

O'Curry, Eugene. *On the Manners and Customs of the Ancient Irish*. Williams and Norgate [London] (1873).

Ó Dónaill, Niall. *Foclóir Gaeilge-Béarla*. An Gúm [Baile Átha Cliath (Dublin)] (1977).

Ó Duinn, Sean. *Rites of Brigid: Goddess and Saint*. Columba Press [Dublin] (2005).

Ó hÓgáin, Dáithí. *Irish Superstitions*. Gill and McMillan [Dublin] (1995).

Ó hÓgáin, Dáithí. *The Lore of Ireland: An Encyclopaedia of Myth, Legend and Romance*. The Collins Press [Cork, Ireland] (2006).

Ó hÓgáin, Dáithí. *The Sacred Isle: Belief and Religion in Pre-Christian Ireland*. Boydell [Woodbridge, England] (1999).

Paterson, T. G. F. "Brigid's Crosses in County Armagh" Ulster Journal of Archaeology, Third Series, Vol. 8 [Belfast] (1945), pp. 43-48.

Plummer, C. *Bethada Náem nÉrenn: Lives of Irish Saints*. Clarendon Press [Oxford] (1922).

Rees, Alwyn and Brinley. *Celtic Heritage: Ancient Tradition in Ireland and Wales*. Thames and Hudson [London] (1961).

Rolleston, T.W. *Myths and Legends of the Celtic Race*. George C. Harrap [London] (1911).

Simms, Katharine. "Bríg Brethach, 'Bríg of the Judgements,'" (undated presentation).

Sjoesdedt, Marie-Louise. *Gods and Heroes of the Celts*. Four Courts Press [Dublin] (1994).

Thompson, Chris and Carmody, Isolde ÓBrolcháin (2016). "Revisiting Mythical Women 05: The Search for Brigid," *Story Archaeology* [podcast]. 12 April 2016 https://storyarchaeology. com/revisiting-mythical-women-05-the-search-for-brigid/ (25 June 2017).

Viney, Michael. *Ireland: A Smithsonian Natural History* (2003).

Wales, Gerald of. See Cambrensis, Giraldus.

Williams, Mark. *Ireland's Immortals: A History of the Gods of Irish Myth*. Princeton University Press (2016).

Wolf, Casey June. *"The Mythical Pairing of Brig and Bres – Its Origins and Meaning in Cath Maige Tuired* (2015). [Like, Brigit, I have several personas. C. J. Wolf is one.] https://www.academia. edu/15429641/The_Mythical_Pairing_of_Brig_and_Bres_Its_ Origins_and_Meaning_in_Cath_Maige_Tuired_Revised_

Wood-Martin, *Traces of the Elder Faiths of Ireland*. Longmans, Green, & Co. [London] (1902).

## Irish Texts

Gray, Elizabeth. (ed. and trans.) *Cath Maige Tuired*. 1983. Irish Text Society [London] (1995). https://celt.ucc.ie//published/ T300010.html

Fraser, J. "The First Battle of Moytura." *Ériu* v.8 (1916), pp. 1-63 [H 2.17] School of Irish Learning [Dublin]. Called *Cath Maige Tuired Cunga*, "The Battle of Moytura" or "The First Battle of

Magh Turedh." http://www.maryjones.us/ctexts/1maghtured.
html

*Lebor Gabála Érenn: Book of the Taking of Ireland* Part 1-5. ed. and
tr. by R. A. S. Macalister. Irish Texts Society [Dublin] (1941).
Better known as "The Book of Invasions." http://www.
maryjones.us/ctexts/leborgabala.html

*Sanas Cormaic* (Cormac's Glossary). Translated and annotated
by John O'Donovan, LL.D. Edited, with notes and indices,
by Whitley Stokes, LL.D. The Irish Archaeological and
Celtic Society [Calcutta](1868). https://archive.org/stream/
sanaschormaicco00stokgoog/sanaschormaicco00stokgoog_
djvu.txt

## Primary Lives of St Brigit

Cogitosus, *Vita II Brigitae* or *Vita Sanctae Brigitae* or "Life of St
Brigit." See "Cogitosus's 'Life of St Brigit' Content and Value"
by Sean Connolly and J.-M. Picard. *The Journal of the Royal
Society of Antiquaries of Ireland* [Dublin], Vol. 117 (1987), pp.
5-27.

*Vita Prima Sanctae Brigitae.* See "Vita Prima Sanctae Brigitae
Background and Historical Value" by Seán Connolly. *The
Journal of the Royal Society of Antiquaries of Ireland* [Dublin],
Vol. 119 (1989), pp. 5-49.

*Bethu Brigte* or the "Irish Life of Saint Brigit:"

*Betha Brigte*: Edited and Translated by Whitley Stokes. *Three
Middle-Irish Homilies on the Lives of Saints Patrick, Brigit and
Columba.* [36 pp.] [Privately printed Calcutta] (1877). https://
celt.ucc.ie//published/G201010/index.html

*Bethu Brigte*: Edited and Translated by Donnchadh Ó hAodha.
Dublin Institute for Advanced Studies (1978). https://celt.ucc.
ie//published/T201002/index.html

"On the Life of St. Brigit," *Leabhar Breac* (*Speckled Book*). Written
in Irish by Murchadh Riabach Ó Cuindlis, A.D. 1408-1411.
Edited and Translated by Whitley Stokes. *Three Middle-Irish*

*Homilies on the Lives of Saints Patrick, Brigit and Columba.* [36 pp.] [Privately printed Calcutta] (1877). Corpus of Electronic Texts Edition: http://publish.ucc.ie/celt/document/T201010

# Resource List

## Reviews

Wolf, Casey June. "A Long Sip at the Well: Brigit Book Reviews" (2014). https://www.academia.edu/10198450/A_Long_Sip_at_the_Well_Brigit_Reviews

## Courses
### *Mael Brigde:*

*Mystery School of the Goddess:*

*Discovering Brigit:* This short course introduces some of the basics of Brigit and assists in going forward in learning about her. http://mysteryschoolofthegoddess.net/2018/05/01/discovering-brigit-goddess-and-saint-with-mael-brigde-open/

*Stepping into Brigit:* This month-long Brigit activation course exposes the participant to more of her lore and traditions while emphasising connecting with Brigit. http://mysteryschoolofthegoddess.net/2017/12/16/stepping-into-brigit-goddess-activation-course-with-mael-brigde-open/

*Journey with Brigit, Goddess of Poetry:* Brigit is your guide and inspiration in this immersion into writing and reading poetry, within the framework of its role in Ireland historically and today. http://mysteryschoolofthegoddess.net/2018/01/21/journey-with-brigit-goddess-of-poetry-with-mael-brigde/

### *Orlagh Costello:*

*The Irish Pagan School:* "Introduction to the Goddess Brigid" https://irishpaganschool.com/p/brighid101

### *Lora O'Brien:*

*The Irish Pagan School:* Learn about Irish Spirituality from a native teacher. Online classes, downloads, blog, tours. https://LoraOBrien.teachable.com/

## Conferences

*Land, Sea, Sky Travel* has hosted three online Brigit conferences to date. Video and audio recordings are available. http://www. landseaskytravel.com or vyviane@landseaskytravel.com

*A Year With Our Gods – Brighid:* (27 January 2018). Hosted by Vyviane Armstrong, opening devotions by Andrea Maxwell. Presenters: Morgan Daimler, Lora O'Brien, Gemma McGowan, Mael Brigde, and Julia Waters.

*Revisiting Brighid – A Year With The Gods Conference:* (26 January 2019). Hosted by Vyviane Armstrong, opening devotions by West Wind Grove. Presenters: Erynn Rowan Laurie, Gemma McGowan, Orlagh Costello, Mael Brigde, Morgan Daimler, and Scealaí Beag (Jon O'Sullivan).

*Brigid – A Friend for the Times:* (16 May 2020). Hosted by Vyviane Armstrong, opening devotions by Vyviane Armstrong. Presenters: Gwilym Morus-Baird, Sage, Alanna, Amy Panetta, Echo Summer, Pauline Rainbow, Mael Brigde.

## Music

This is just the tiniest taste of music sung in Brigit's honour:

Canty. *Flame of Ireland – Medieval Irish Plainchant: An Office for St. Brigit.* ASV Gaudeamus (2005). Out of print; to be rereleased.

Mael Brigde. *SoundCloud.* https://soundcloud.com/user-617834076

Minogue, Áine. "Gabhaim Molta Bríde (We Praise Brigid)," *Circle of the Sun.* RCA (2000).

Singing the Land (Ní Chiardha, Elaine). "Brigid of the Flame." *SoundCloud.* https://soundcloud.com/singingtheland/brigid-of-the-flame

Taylor, Katy. *Welcome Brigid.* CD Baby (2005).

# Brigit-Focussed Groups
## Catholic Brigidine Sisters
*Solas Bhride Centre and Hermitages:* (Ireland) http://solasbhride.ie
*Brigidine Sisters:* (Australia) http://www.brigidine.org.au
*Brigidine Asylum Seekers Project (BASP):* http://basp.org.au
*Brigidine Sisters:* (New Zealand) http://www.brigidine.org.nz

## Brigit Group (Non-Flame-Tending)
(There are several on Facebook and elsewhere, so look around).
*Brighid's Flame:* (Melinda Taylor Kelly. Open to "all devotees of Brighid, from all traditions.") https://www.facebook.com/groups/brighidsflame/
*Brigid's Forge:* (Orlagh Costello. Open to Neo-Pagan, Christian, etc., honouring both goddess and saint). https://www.facebook.com/groups/318562765289760/?ref=bookmarks
*Cairde Bhride (Friends of Brigid):* (Associated with the Brigidine Sisters, they are "people enlivened by the Brigid tradition who share common interests based on a view of society that is inclusive and founded on right relationships.") http://www.kildaracentre.org/cairde_bhride/index.html
*Clann Bhríde Facebook Group*: (Open to non-members and members of the flamekeeping cill). https://www.facebook.com/groups/clannbhride/

## Flame-Tending Groups
*Clann Bhride (Children of Brighid) Flamekeeping Cill:* https://clannbhride.org/fellowship/clann-bhride-cill/
*Daughters of the Flame:* (Women only). http://www.obsidianmagazine.com/DaughtersoftheFlame/
*Ord Brighideach:* http://www.ordbrighideach.org/raven/
*The Flame Keepers of Holy Bride:* (The Holy Celtic Order of the Temple) Offers a Liberal Catholic path to esoteric knowledge and mystical experience. Connected with St. Gall's Retreat in Switzerland https://tinyurl.com/yxbkyxyo

*Sanctuary of Brigid:* (Women only). *https://www.sanctuaryofbrigid. com/flamekeepers/*

## Pilgrimages and Festivals

*Brigid of Faughart Festival – A Celebration of Brigid, Goddess and Saint:* www.brigidoffaughart.ie
*Brigid's Way Pilgrimage – An Ancient Path Between Sky and Earth:* http://brigidsway.ie
*Féile Bríde* (Festival of St. Brigid): http://solasbhride.ie

## Online Resources (Brigit)
*Brighid, Goddess and Saint:* (Paul Williment) https://brighid.org. uk
*Brigit's Forge:* (Hilaire Wood) http://www.brigitsforge.co.uk
*Brigit's Sparkling Flame:* (Mael Brigde: General Brigit postings) http://brigitssparklingflame.blogspot.ca
*Her Eternal Flame: Contemplative Brighidine Mysticism:* (Erin Nighean Brìghde) https://hereternalflame.wordpress.com
"St. Brigit of Ireland: From Virgin Saint to Fertility Goddess:" (Lisa M. Bitel) How Brigit may have become a goddess secondarily. This does not negate the presence of sovereignty goddesses in Irish mythology, or necessarily refute a Brig/ Brigit who precedes the saint. http://monasticmatrix.osu.edu/ commentaria/st-brigit-ireland
"Redeeming Holy Days Candlemas Presentation:" http:// steadfastlutherans.org/2015/01/redeeming-holy-days-candlemaspresentation-2/
*Stone on the Belly:* (Mael Brigde: Brigit poetry blog). http:// stonebelly.blogspot.com
"The Mythical Pairing of Brig and Bres: Its Origins and Meaning in Cath Maige Tuired (Revised):" (Casey June Wolf (2015)). https://www.academia.edu/15429641/The_Mythical_Pairing_ of_Brig_and_Bres_Its_Origins_and_Meaning_in_Cath_

Maige_Tuired_Revised_
*Story Archaeology:* "Revisiting Mythical Women 05: The Search for Brigid." https://storyarchaeology.com/revisiting-mythical-women-05-the-search-for-brigid/
*Trias Thaumaturga*: (Marcella: blog on the three patron saints of Ireland). Contains numerous informative and well considered posts on Saint Brigit. http://triasthaumaturga.blogspot.com
*Virtual Shrine of Brighid:* (Order of WhiteOak/Ord na Darach Gile) http://www.celticheritage.co.uk/virtualshrine/

## Online Resources (General)

*CELT:* (University College Cork) Online resource for original Irish texts. http://www.ucc.ie/celt/
*Celtic Feminine Podcast – At the Cross-Section Between Folklore, Ethnomusicology, Women's Studies, and Celtic Spirituality:* (Amy Panetta) https://www.thecelticfemininepodcast.com
*Celtic Literature Collective:* (Mary Jones) http://www.maryjones.us/ctexts/index_irish.html
*Irish-American Witchcraft: Irish Pagan Resources:* (Morgan Daimler: Morgan's great list of books, blogs, and things to bear in mind) in *Patheos* 5 February 2019 https://www.patheos.com/blogs/agora/2019/02/irish-pagan-resources/?utm_medium=social&utm_source=share_bar
*Irish Reconstructionist Polytheism:* (Morgan Daimler) http://sidhemoonwitch.wix.com/irishpolytheism
*Story Archaeology:* Uncovering the layers of Irish Mythology. http://storyarchaeology.com
*Tairis:* (Annie Loughlin) Good grounding in Celtic Gods from a Scottish perspective, including "The Gaelic Year," (2006-2018). http://www.tairis.co.uk
*The Schools' Collection:* (Dúchas) Folklore collected by the school children of Ireland from their elders. https://www.duchas.ie/en/cbes

# About the Author

In late 1992, Mael Brigde founded Daughters of the Flame, an international, interfaith Brigidine flame-keeping group for women. Her aim was to rekindle the perpetual flame burned by Saint Brigit's order in Kildare, Ireland until the 1600s. She lit their initiatory candle on Imbolc 1993, unaware that on that same day in Kildare the Catholic Brigidine Sisters were also relighting her flame.

Mael Brigde publishes a general interest Brigit blog, *Brigit's Sparkling Flame* (2004), and a Brigit poetry blog, *Stone on the Belly* (2015). She is widely read in Brigidine literature and her paper, "A Long Sip at the Well," reviews dozens of Brigidine books, from children's picture books through popular nonfiction, poetry, plays, and novels to academic texts. Another paper, "The Mythical Pairing of Brig and Bres: Its Origins and Meaning in Cath Maige Tuired," discusses among other things the case for Brigit as sovereignty goddess. Both are available on *Brigit's Sparkling Flame* and *Academia.edu*.

In addition to maintaining the Daughters of the Flame and her blogs, Mael Brigde has contributed Brigidine essays and poems to a number of books, assisted others in their researches, led webinars on Brigit and Brigidine devotion, and created three online classes for those wishing to learn more about Brigit and grow closer to her. The first, *Discovering Brigit*, introduces Brigit and many of the ideas associated with her. The second, *Stepping into Brigit*, guides the seeker into a deepening connection with her. The third, *Journey with Brigit, Goddess of Poetry*, is a longer, intensive class that explores reading and writing poetry as a sacred act, offering meditations, historical information, and the model of both ancient and modern Irish poets.

Mael Brigde lives in Vancouver, Canada.

# Author Links

Thank you for purchasing *A Brigit of Ireland Devotional – Sun Among Stars*. I hope it has contributed in some way to your understanding of Brigit or your devotion to her, as its creation has enhanced my own. If you have a few moments, please feel free to add a review of the book to your favorite online site. You are welcome to be in touch through any of the following links.

Sweet blessings of Brigit on you.

Mael Brigde

## Daughters of the Flame

http://www.obsidianmagazine.com/DaughtersoftheFlame/index.htm

## Blogs

*Brigit's Sparkling Flame (General):* http://brigitssparklingflame.blogspot.com/

*Stone on the Belly (Brigit Poetry):* http://stonebelly.blogspot.ca/

## Facebook Profile

https://www.facebook.com/mael.brigde

## Brigit's Portal: Classes, Gatherings, Poetry, Tools

https://www.facebook.com/BrigitsPortal/

## Twitter

https://twitter.com/MaelBrigde

## Soundcloud

https://soundcloud.com/user-617834076

## Online Courses

Discovering Brigit (Introductory):
http://mysteryschoolofthegoddess.net/2017/12/16/discovering-brigit-goddess-and-saint-with-mael-brigde-open/

*Stepping into Brigit (Goddess Activation):*
http://mysteryschoolofthegoddess.net/2017/12/16/stepping-into-brigit-goddess-activation-course-with-mael-brigde-open/

Journey with Brigit, Goddess of Poetry (Immersion Course):
http://mysteryschoolofthegoddess.net/2018/01/21/journey-with-brigit-goddess-of-poetry-with-mael-brigde/

## Conference Recordings

See Conferences in the Resource List for information on obtaining them from Land, Sea, Sky Travel.

## Papers

(writing as Casey June Wolf)
"A Long Sip at the Well" (Brigit book reviews):
https://www.academia.edu/10198450/A_Long_Sip_at_the_Well_Brigit_Reviews

"The Mythical Pairing of Brig and Bres: Its Origins and Meaning in Cath Maige Tuired *(Revised)*":
https://www.academia.edu/15429641/The_Mythical_Pairing_of_Brig_and_Bres_Its_Origins_and_Meaning_in_Cath_Maige_Tuired_Revised_

## Interview

Panetta, Amy. "Mael Brigde, Founder of the 'Brigit's Sparkling Flame' Blog and 'Daughters of the Flame' Flametending Group, Discusses Her Work," *Celtic Feminine Podcast* (March 8, 2018). https://www.thecelticfemininepodcast.com/single-post/2018/

03/08/Mael-Brigde-Founder-of-the-Brigits-Sparkling-Flame-
Blog-and-Daughters-of-the-Flame-Flametending-Group-
Discusses-Her-Work

# Previous Book

*Finding Creatures & Other Stories,* under the name C. June Wolf.
Wattle and Daub Books (2008). ISBN 0981065805

Literary, science fictional, slipstream, and fantastic – this medley
of stories is grounded in the present day, weaving back to the life
of Saint Francis, and forward to a time when Earth is a memory
and new humans are finding their place among the stars.

A Haitian street kid with a mercurial coin, a skid row waitress
with a passion for palaeontology, aliens trapped in sculptures
by Henry Moore – these journey alongside a First Nations
elder confronting harsh memories as he brings peace to a dead
spaceman, and two teenagers who build an old-style science
fiction machine with a very modern purpose.

Wolf's unexpected approach to story-telling interlaces
humour and compassion with a fine-spun unorthodoxy in these
understated tales of this world and beyond.

"Wolf uses different genres, different voices, different cultures –
in short whatever she needs to make the story work. What ties it
all together is her sure-handed prose and a depth she brings to

her writing, that indefinable element that rises up from between the lines and gives a good story its resonance...

"I found the characters and their situations kept bubbling up from my memory, so that I'd be standing in a check-out line, or washing the dishes, and find myself thinking about this character, that situation, that particular turn of phrase.

"If you're reading this, you've probably already the bought the book, so rather than my trying to convince you to buy it, let me ask you instead to pass it around when you're done. Talk about the stories that moved you, about Wolf's voice, and her gift of storytelling." from his introduction to *Finding Creatures & Other Stories,* **Charles de Lint**, author of *Moonheart* and *The Wind in His Heart*; winner of the World Fantasy Award (2000) for his collection, *Moonlight and Vines*

Copies of *Finding Creatures & Other Stories* are available from Mael Brigde.

# Acknowledgements

*Sun Among Stars* has been long years in the making, and over that time many people have helped to make it both possible and rewarding for me to continue with it. I am enormously grateful to them all.

For her many (and not always immediately obvious!) blessings and continuing inspiration, I thank Brigit.

For tending her flame and working for peace and reconciliation, I thank the Brigidine nuns. Sisters Mary Minehan and Phil O'Shea of Solas Bhríde I thank especially for extending a warm welcome to me long ago and for being so respectful of my Neo-Pagan path. This gift had a great impact on my spiritual life.

For her passionate enthusiasm for these poems and the memories they evoked of her childhood in Kildare, I thank Irene Shirley. When I questioned whether I, who had not been raised in Ireland, should be writing them, she showed me how much they meant to her, and urged me to carry on.

I am deeply grateful to the scholars whose works I have relied upon, with all their differing conclusions, and to the Neo-Pagan and Brigit communities for answering – and asking – countless questions and being companions on this journey.

I thank Anne Key (Goddess Ink) and Kimberley Moore (Mystery School of the Goddess) for giving me a means to offer Brigit courses, and to Vyviane Armstrong (Land, Sea, Sky Travel) for inviting me to teach at her online Brigit conferences. To the participants in my classes who have shared their insights and inspirations: I am blessed by your generosity.

I thank Erynn Rowan Laurie, who took my ardour for Brigit seriously early on, and who encouraged and supported me in my devotion to and understanding of her throughout the years, directly and through her own research and writings.

My inexpressible thanks go to the Daughters of the Flame, past and present, who have lived this devotion with me for decades. Your presence has shaped my life. Special thanks to Ani Greenwood, Erynn Rowan Laurie, Donna Amaral, Josie Davey, Lily Miller, Gail Nyoka, and Nichole Cardillo for your support of me in my role of chief cook and bottle washer to the Daughters.

To my sister in Bride, Heather Upfield, who touches my heart and tends with me our shared contemplative, lay monastic vision: thank you, dear fellow hermit.

Warm thanks to Morgan Daimler and Orlagh Costello for taking the time to think with me about Brigit, for their written contributions to this book, and for their own diligent and heartfelt offerings to the community.

Those who contributed to the nurturing, polishing, and presentation of these writings, the members of the Kyle and Shadbolt writing classes, my mentor and friend, Eileen Kernaghan, my wonderful editor and friend, Clélie Rich, I give great thanks for your endless encouragement, thoughtful critiques, and unflagging generosity.

Finally, eternal thanks to Kelly Johnson, Kathryn Boegel, Susan Pinkus, and Lorraine Arnott, who have always respected my relationship with Brigit, and behaved as though my writing really mattered to them.

My sincere apologies to anyone I have overlooked on this page.

Go raibh mile maith agaibh go leir.

**MOON
BOOKS**

## PAGANISM & SHAMANISM

What is Paganism? A religion, a spirituality, an alternative belief system, nature worship? You can find support for all these definitions (and many more) in dictionaries, encyclopaedias, and text books of religion, but subscribe to any one and the truth will evade you. Above all Paganism is a creative pursuit, an encounter with reality, an exploration of meaning and an expression of the soul. Druids, Heathens, Wiccans and others, all contribute their insights and literary riches to the Pagan tradition. Moon Books invites you to begin or to deepen your own encounter, right here, right now. If you have enjoyed this book, why not tell other readers by posting a review on your preferred book site.

## Recent bestsellers from Moon Books are:

### Journey to the Dark Goddess
How to Return to Your Soul
Jane Meredith
Discover the powerful secrets of the Dark Goddess and
transform your depression, grief and pain into healing
and integration.
Paperback: 978-1-84694-677-6 ebook: 978-1-78099-223-5

### Shamanic Reiki
Expanded Ways of Working with Universal Life Force Energy
Llyn Roberts, Robert Levy
Shamanism and Reiki are each powerful ways of healing; together,
their power multiplies. *Shamanic Reiki* introduces techniques to
help healers and Reiki practitioners tap ancient healing wisdom.
Paperback: 978-1-84694-037-8 ebook: 978-1-84694-650-9

### Pagan Portals – The Awen Alone
Walking the Path of the Solitary Druid
Joanna van der Hoeven
An introductory guide for the solitary Druid, *The Awen Alone* will
accompany you as you explore, and seek out your own place
within the natural world.
Paperback: 978-1-78279-547-6 ebook: 978-1-78279-546-9

### A Kitchen Witch's World of Magical Herbs & Plants
Rachel Patterson
A journey into the magical world of herbs and plants, filled with
magical uses, folklore, history and practical magic. By popular
writer, blogger and kitchen witch, Tansy Firedragon.
Paperback: 978-1-78279-621-3 ebook: 978-1-78279-620-6

**Medicine for the Soul**
The Complete Book of Shamanic Healing
Ross Heaven
All you will ever need to know about shamanic healing and how to
become your own shaman...
Paperback: 978-1-78099-419-2 ebook: 978-1-78099-420-8


**Shaman Pathways – The Druid Shaman**
Exploring the Celtic Otherworld
Danu Forest
A practical guide to Celtic shamanism with exercises and
techniques as well as traditional lore for exploring the Celtic
Otherworld.
Paperback: 978-1-78099-615-8 ebook: 978-1-78099-616-5


**Traditional Witchcraft for the Woods and Forests**
A Witch's Guide to the Woodland with Guided Meditations and
Pathworking
Mélusine Draco
A Witch's guide to walking alone in the woods, with guided
meditations and pathworking.
Paperback: 978-1-84694-803-9 ebook: 978-1-84694-804-6


**Naming the Goddess**
Trevor Greenfield
*Naming the Goddess* is written by over eighty adherents and
scholars of Goddess and Goddess Spirituality.
Paperback: 978-1-78279-476-9 ebook: 978-1-78279-475-2

**Shapeshifting into Higher Consciousness**
Heal and Transform Yourself and Our World with Ancient
Shamanic and Modern Methods
Llyn Roberts
Ancient and modern methods that you can use every day to
transform yourself and make a positive difference in the world.
Paperback: 978-1-84694-843-5 ebook: 978-1-84694-844-2

Readers of ebooks can buy or view any of these bestsellers by
clicking on the live link in the title. Most titles are published in
paperback and as an ebook. Paperbacks are available in traditional
bookshops. Both print and ebook formats are available online.

Find more titles and sign up to our readers' newsletter at
http://www.johnhuntpublishing.com/paganism
Follow us on Facebook at https://www.facebook.com/MoonBooks
and Twitter at https://twitter.com/MoonBooksJHP